If Only...
Life Lessons Learned

14 TRANSFORMATIONAL STORIES

Contributing Authors:

Yvonne Anello, Veronica Bishop, Jennifer Blakley, Abigail Bruce, Jeanette Emmons, Michelle Barry Franco, Richard Gear, Danea Horn, Kristen Karle, Feroshia Knight, Ben Luskin, Melanie McCloskey, Mary Sommerset, and Suzanne Shafer

published by The Baraka Institute & Coach Training World
www.barakainstitute.com

Edited by Laura Whittemore | Book Design by Agent 47, LLC

ISBN: 978-0615575056

Dedication

The book is devoted to you!

Thank you for joining us as we
find our way... together!

14 Transformational Stories

Acknowledgements

More than a village, it was pure heart and soul that made this collaborative book possible. In particular, I'd like to thank the following individuals for their efforts, energy, enthusiasm, and support in making this project a reality: Carrie Ure, for her mentoring of our contributors; Kim Tally, without whom Baraka Institute would not exist; my incredibly talented book project manager Kristen Karle; Geordie Humphrey for his detailed attention in the layout process; Laura Whittemore our fearless editor whose loving red marks were ever so appreciated and lastly, my faithful dog, MoChee, who sat by many an hour, dutifully watching me and wondering if I would ever take him outside again.

And of course, I'd like to thank again our contributors who devoted their hearts and souls to the project and put their trust in me to bring this book to fruition: Yvonne Anello, Veronica Bishop, Jennifer Blakley, Abigail Bruce, Jeanette Emmons, Michelle Barry Franco, Richard Gear, Danea Horn, Kristen Karle, Ben Luskin, Melanie McCloskey, Mary Sommerset, and Suzanne Shafer.

And to all the other *Change Artists* who continue to inspire me with their work, wisdom and devotion to the art and science of making a difference in the world.

Lastly, extra special thanks to my long-term supporters and champions Tina Roe, Michelle Wirta, Soren Sorenson, Jerry Henderson, Laura Joki, and Dawn Farr who helped me shape the future of Baraka Institute by sharing their minds, hearts, and skills over the years.

I adore and love you all.

Feroshia Knight, MA, PCC
Founder & Executive Director
Baraka Institute: Leadership Development & Accredited Coach Training Center

Preface

Riding along the jagged edge of the California coastline, I felt the jerking sway of the train. The stop-start-stop-start pattern, combined with the serpentine flow of high-speed transit, was strangely comforting to me.

On the one hand, I knew I wasn't in control—my least favorite position—and trains, when they wreck, tend to do so in spectacular fashion; but I felt safe with the numerous stations along the way where I could easily step off and plant my feet on solid ground. Much like the speed of life, I knew I could put on the brakes and regain some measure of control. On the other hand, being essentially held captive on a speeding bullet offered a treasure chest of precious hours I normally don't give myself to focus on my work, especially my writing. In my life, *I* am usually the speeding bullet, allowing myself few stops.

While on these numerous train rides, I'd often lounge in the spacious dining car reminiscent of my atrium tree house nestled in the woods. I felt at home in this space. I'd plug in my Macintosh, have a bite to eat, and experience the broadest strokes of scenery through the expansive windows. More importantly, I came in direct contact with nearly everyone passing through the dining car, with plenty of opportunity to meet interesting people on these long and lonely journeys.

It was on an early morning, close to my final destination that a young boy with deep-set brown eyes approached me. He was seven at most, with a ravenous appetite for information. After lobbing a basketful of questions at me, including "Is that your real hair color?" (God, that gets old…), "How old are you?" and a few more probing inquiries, he blurted out one that struck me hard: "What is life?"

I was stunned, because it's the adults in my professional world who always ask about the meaning of life and their purpose in it, along with the omnipresent "What am I supposed to be when I grow up?" But in that moment, I couldn't believe a seven-year-old, a little person of such innocence and purity, could stump me. Considering that I was the supposedly knowledgeable adult and he was the naïve child, I felt like I needed to offer up some sort of meaningful answer.

I mentally flipped through my vast resources, searching for the right words while concerned that my wisdom might land on his absorbent ears in ways I couldn't predict. In hindsight, my jaded viewpoint may not have been the best launching point. After all, "Love of My Life #3" had recently revealed himself to be another figment of my imagination, instilling me with said jaded viewpoint. A harsh reality had taken hold when #3 had walked away with a younger woman and left me crushed. But none of that was important for this young boy to know, and I bit my tongue as I carefully chose a reply.

"Life is simple," I said. "It's nothing more than a string of events and situations that we participate in, often by conscious choice and sometimes unconsciously by default or while on autopilot. These experiences begin to shape our lives and frame who we are, what we want, why we want it, and how we will live each day from here on out."

As the last words slipped through my lips, I could hear my inner critic screaming, "Really? Really, Feroshia? You're speaking to a young kid – he'll never get any of that!"

And that critic was so right. The heartfelt sentiment I normally reserved for those old enough to have gainful employment landed far afield of my young target. The smug smile across my face rapidly melted, and my heart pounded in embarrassment at not knowing how to frame an appropriate answer for a kid. His expression said it all.

But a curious mind never stops, and within seconds the boy responded with yet another attempt to learn.

"What does *conscious* mean?"

In my work, I'm normally cautious about how my presence impacts others. And if I'm honest, I too want to belong and feel included. When you're a entering a new coaching relationship, there's always that initial period in which you must create trust with your client before any progress can be made. Through the years, I've discovered that trust cannot be jump-started via a deep conversation about the meaning of life—especially through an over-intellectualized lens. But here I was, caught off-guard and cornered by a seven-year-old.

From the corner of my eye, I saw relief in sight. A parental figure walked through the compartment door, and I hoped this conversation would end as abruptly as a pair of authoritative hands could scoop up my inquisitor. After all, I reminded myself, these kinds of conversations are a parent's duty, not a stranger's—even one like me with expertise and an affinity for helping others navigate the oft-rough and complicated waters of life. I figured this was especially true when a young boy speaks to a middle-aged, emotionally disrupted, broken-hearted woman. But to my dismay, the adult walked past, without so much as a glance.

"Hello!" he prodded me, "I asked you, what does 'conscious' mean?"

His impatience was all too familiar to me—from my work and from my own explorations of life. I looked into his eyes and felt a sudden emotional urge to rain down on him like a heavy gray cloud bursting over the arid earth below. He demanded answers, and I, quite egotistically, thought I was just the person to quench his thirst for knowledge.

The thoughts swirled through my brain, what if I could give him my lessons learned? Could I prevent him from living the life I had? The sadness and frustration? Those moments of deep pain that I thought I'd never survive? Could I help him understand that self-esteem, confidence, and courage should have been my best friends, far and above those peers and colleagues who I instead tried so hard to please? Should I forewarn him that his heart might be broken more than once? Or should I share my secrets on how to maximize his potential, to live life to the fullest—encourage him to be his best self and live his dream life? Should I share insights about how being a good listener and learner will win him rewarding relationships and the kind of success many seek? How could I share every lesson I had learned so that he might have an advantage over the worst life could throw at him—that knowledge I didn't have as a child—would it change his life for the better?

My ego was aided and abetted by the real pain I had suffered, along with the vivid and visceral memories of things I had slammed face-first into. However, I quickly realized not only wouldn't he understand, my words would have very little meaning to his world—especially coming from a stranger who knew nothing about him. So I tossed out the simplest answer I could:

"Consciousness means that you are present in the moment—curious and self-aware."

"I'm self-aware!" yelped the excited youngster, "My mom tells me so! She says I am always evolving, and that I should be curious and open and live life fully. She says curiosity and learning are the keys to finding success in all parts of your life. I know I want to be a jet plane pilot. I want two kids, both girls, and, of course, a wife. I want to live in New York City and fly to France like my dad does…"

His impassioned little voice expelled words of wisdom that modeled those I would have spouted, given the chance. Challenged by his cleverness, I responded, "So how do you know this to be true?"

He pointed to his heart. "I just do. It comes from inside. I know this because I can feel it."

A grin spread across his face, and I admit it brought a tear to my eyes. He already knew what it took me decades to discover. I wanted so much to thank his mother for giving such a precious gift of self-possession to this young boy. I wondered when she would walk through that door and come for him, and glanced toward it in anticipation.

"Good" I said. "I'm happy to hear that you have such a clear idea of who you want to be and how you will know it when you've arrived. Son, that brings a lot of joy to me, and I know someday I'll be remembering this conversation—and you—because it's been a very meaningful one for me."

Then with one exhale of air, the young man dashed from my presence, through the door to the next train compartment. I was momentarily stunned by our interactions.

Immediately, my vocal inner critic came out to play. What if I had been so self-aware at his young age? Who would I be today? I don't remember knowing anything of what I wanted—definitely not with the detail and passion he had displayed. What if I'd had conversations with my parents and mentors that fostered my own consciousness and self-awareness? Wow, what an incredible gift that would have been!

I couldn't let it go. If only I'd had someone in my life that held such a positive outlook about how to be my best self from the get-go? If only I had known these things in my life.

Even though I wanted to be more helpful in preparing that boy, I realized that my agenda was about me—my need to help, to teach, to guide, to be of value in the eyes and minds of others. Despite this hunger to be useful, I've since learned to embrace my desire to be of service and a change-maker in the world as part of the person in me that needs managing. Truly, a big difference lies between being asked to help and laying one's own life framework down on others. Such unsolicited advice often falls far from others' ears and is rarely on target for anyone other than the person doling out the advice.

The Birth of Baraka Institute

It's often true that the littlest things will have the greatest impact. In 2005, years after the incident with the boy on the train, I opened doors to the Baraka Institute. Steve, one of my subcontractors at my marketing agency, Agent 47, LCC, suggested the name. The meaning of Baraka resonated deeply with what he believed to be my mission.

> The Sufi translation reads: "Baraka, also *berakhah*, in Judaism, a blessing usually recited during a ceremony." Baraka, also *barakah*, in Arabic Islam and Arabic-influenced languages such as Swahili, Urdu, Persian, Turkish, is a blessing from God in the form of spiritual wisdom or divine presence; also a spiritual power believed to be possessed by certain persons, objects, tombs.

I didn't understand Steve's connection at first, and more importantly, I didn't want to own the responsibility for such a magnanimous label. But I did love the way "Ba_Rah_Kah" sounded tribal when pronounced. I'm a profound lover of music, especially tribal beats, and I enjoyed repeating that word often. Eventually, I overcame my fear of the name and embraced it as a good representation of my purpose. And who would have thought that a few years later our first black president would be named Barack Obama?

Supported by a few colleagues and friends, I launched Baraka

Institute's first publicly offered professional development courses. Much of this material was developed and adapted from the previous decade of work in leadership development, team building, communication, business development, and, in particular, the area of human strategy and development.

I had grown especially fond of cultivating self-awareness as a key element for business success. A decade of experience in a successful marketing and communications agency had taught me that behind every transaction was a human; and that the more conscious and self-aware the company and its people were about things that mattered most to them, both personally and in business (values, mission, purpose etc.), the more the company would thrive.

Initially, convincing others of this concept as a guiding principle was challenging, but since the early nineties, much has changed. Therefore, I am thankful for the thoughtful leaders and organizational experts who shared a similar view and the resulting professional books on the subject that created a tipping point in support of organization and leadership coaching. Our profession is growing and developing at lightning speeds.

My earlier work with leaders and their teams was shaped by my role as a "fire fighter." I possessed an infectious energy–or perhaps it was my Pollyanna outlook, as diagnosed by a few skeptics. With that energy, I was poised to take on the harder conversations and riskier conflict-rich environments. I had become comfortable asking tough questions that evoked answers people didn't know existed inside them. Once revealed, these answers provided insights that helped leaders and their teams release unproductive patterns they'd held onto for years. They shifted attitudes and approaches, and moved toward more effective and happier workplaces as a result.

My prime goal was to create peace and unity within organizations where their productivity and happiness had been undermined by ineffective communication and sabotaging behaviors. These patterns were not only impacting their success, but mine as well and as their strategic marketing and business development consultant I took a personal interest in helping them see another way to connect, collaborate and co-create in the workplace.

Having begun my corporate relationships in a marketing and communications agency, I easily shifted from the role of marketer to human strategist—and at times, to the role of "fire fighter." My successful efforts earned me long-term relationships and a reputation as a corporate "shaman." My ability to help others evolved from conflict resolution to the lighter side of team building, visioning, and creating a preferred future for all involved. Even the toughest of board, team, and sales meetings became productive and proactive in nature. Leaders found new ways to influence their people, and they themselves reconnected to their own purposes and passions in and outside of their companies.

All around me, leaders were fascinated by my methods. I was called "unstoppable, with an endless flow of positivity." Many would ask how I could source that out. I would laugh a little self-consciously when they'd remark how great it would be if they could box up my gift and take it home. I could only imagine what problems they really wanted to cure.

Through my work, I discovered the unhappiness that existed behind closed doors. I wondered how many of these individuals were like me, wishing they had a guide or mentor to show them the way when dealing with the unknown and unpredictable nature of life and business. I took the discoveries as a sign I could make a difference in peoples' lives and in their businesses. But I knew I couldn't do it alone. Operating in the heat of conflict and human complexity is no easy feat.

I sought camaraderie in tackling the vastness of change-making in corporate land and in the world as a whole. Baraka Institute was birthed as the place from which I could foster an army of change agents: others who, like me, felt empowered to step into unfamiliar territories and address human complexities, helping grow both business and new human potential or reinvigorate life that had seemed to die years ago. It has been a dream come true to have ongoing meaningful relationships with some of the best-hearted individuals on the planet. With Baraka, I found the family I had always looked for, a family of change agents, coaches, and mentors; I would do anything to keep it well-supported and growing.

One of the key principles at Baraka Institute is the importance of "wholeness and the unity of one's relationship to self, others, and the world as a whole." Through a self-discovery process, we explore *who* our clients are by identifying and honoring the roles and personas they assume in the various parts of their life, such as mother, leader, learner, cynic, free spirit, artist. In combination, these roles and personas make up their Signature Self. Knowing *who* you are in connection with *what* matters most and the *why* behind it helps both client and coach to separate the story from the storyteller. It's often in our own story that we get lost—separated from reality because our imaginations can run wild. It is when we are not living the truth or refusing to accept reality that our worlds can become unpredictable and challenging. Those inaccurate beliefs and fears lead us astray—always, every time.

As part of a training and development process, our change agents are well equipped to help others understand how their thoughts, feelings, and actions create reality and that all parts of our life contribute to the success of our life as a whole.

My hard lesson learned: even those who teach, coach, and make a difference in the lives of others can fail. We have to stay conscious, awake, and aware of what *is*. We have to know our own truths, that overextending ourselves and self-sacrificing—even for the greater good—will make an impact and have consequences; even though we may be spending countless hours as pioneers and adventurers, we don't have to go it alone. We don't have to light the path for others all by ourselves.

When things seemed the brightest in my career, I hadn't realized that I had become my own slave. My devotion to making the biggest impact possible was all consuming and I relinquished my own desires for a personal relationship and family, subordinating them to the organization I worked so hard to make a success. With a tunnel-vision focus, I lost sight of myself. My health rapidly declined, as well as my sense of adventure and fun, while I dedicated all my energy to the Institute and those it supported. My deep desire to be of service—to be the fire fighter, leader, learner, guide, mentor, coach, and do-it-all-yourselfer all rolled into one—was disabling me. I wasn't the good role model I had aspired to be. In my attempts to be all things to all people, I forgot that work, even though it was the most visibly rewarded aspect of my life, wasn't the whole of my life. That infectious energy I was so highly praised for began to dwindle, and though I could sustain the fast pace for brief amounts of time, it became obvious through my physical deterioration that a personal course change was essential.

Eventually, I found my way and learned yet another hard lesson about life—the very one I teach in leadership today: *Together is better.* Baraka Institute could not be sustained on my good efforts alone. We needed more than the support of a small team – *we need a village!*

As a constant reminder to stay in balance and wholeness, I am fond of metaphorically first putting on your own air mask first before assisting others. No wonder this message bears particular importance every time you get on a flight. What a beautiful reminder about the meaning of self-care and love. When you self-sabotage—consciously or not—your efforts cannot be sustained. Eventually, something will have to give, usually as a result of feeling too much pain.

Remember that no one needs to go through life alone. Part of my journey through self-discovery, and as the founding leader among many other new and seasoned leaders, is the belief that the most powerful way to exist is in relationship. Not only do others help us to see ourselves better but the connection we share with others makes life much more doable and fun along the way.

From my most anguished and hardest-won life lessons, my deepest desire emerged: the desire to fully collaborate with and support others as they showed up and shined at helping even more people.

About the Authors

As part of my commitment to our community and to the coaching and mentoring profession, it's been a dream come true to produce media: books, DVDs, online training, and development curriculum that represent the whole of Baraka Institute, including the validation of our many graduates and program attendees. As a result, our agents of change (or change artists) at Baraka Institute not only coach, but they communicate, teach, speak, write, and spread our most valued concepts to the world – concepts that when embraced can change everything about one's life at work, home and play.

It is with great pride that as part of our expanding collaborative efforts we are able to bring to you fourteen of our certified Whole Person Coaches and ICF Credentialed Coaches, ready to share their lessons learned to help you navigate your life in the best way possible.

The stories in this book are real. Many of the authors have felt vulnerable in making these stories public. However, they speak their truths in the hopes that you as the reader will relate to and benefit from our shared human experience—the good and not so good. It is only because we have conquered our own life challenges, and continue to manage our lives more effectively, that we can come to you and divulge so much of ourselves.

We all share the desire for love, unity, understanding, trust, and peace. We all long to be part of something bigger than ourselves. We all want to believe we can always reach out safely for the support we deserve and, in return, be good and caring role models for others. It has been a great honor to be part of this community, and I believe the reason you are reading this book may have something to do with your own calling to be of service or a calling to do what it takes to help yourself live your best life.

Many of the themes found throughout this book reflect the proverbial questions, "If only…" and "What if?" They relate some of our life-changing moments that would have been so much easier to understand and endure if only we'd had a little more support, guidance, or experience to help us navigate more effectively. You will hear many of us asking questions as part of our learning and self-discovery process.

Before we realized our truths and got the support we needed, we could fill in the blanks with every worst-case scenario our imaginations could concoct. Some of us even made a regular habit of doing just that and keeping ourselves mired in fear and inaction. We held ourselves in contempt of our own lives, refrained from taking courageous chances, and didn't allow ourselves the joy of living life to the fullest. Today, though, we are coming to you with some of *those* lessons learned.

At Baraka, we believe it's never too late to learn and lead a life full of happiness and joy! We recognize there are still more lessons to come and that we are in this together, as we continue to find our way. And this is our invitation for you to share this journey with us!

And in deep gratitude, here's my final toast to the seven-year-old boy who made such a difference in my life: May you be the brightest star ever, wherever you shine. And thank you, #3: If things hadn't played out the way they did, I would not have been on that train. Things do happen for a reason.

*"Finally, brothers, whatever is true, whatever is noble, whatever is right,
whatever is pure, whatever is lovely, whatever is admirable
– if anything is excellent or praiseworthy
– think about such things."
~ Philippians 4: 6-8*

Paved with Good INTENTIONS

by Abigail Bruce

I want to state at the outset that nowhere in this recounting do I intend to put down my family, my church, Christianity or religion in general. I now understand there are many who, identifying with my past and my upbringing, nevertheless did not struggle as I did. I also believe that everything happens for a reason and that everything works together for good. My story has everything to do with my personality, and my childhood and religious experience have contributed to the person I am today. I'm not perfect, but I am peaceful. This is a story about the journey I took from fear and anxiety to peace and wholeness.

Belief

Both my parents are religious people. Dad is a minister and Mom is not only a minister's wife but a minister's daughter as well. My four younger siblings and I were raised in a conservative home, as Seventh Day Baptists, which elicited lots of questions about why went to church on Saturday. We got a lot of the "you're weird," and "I don't get that" kinds of stares.

On the one hand, I never particularly cared what people thought of who I was or what I did. When others questioned my religious belief, I was more than happy to explain it to them, whether or not they agreed. And yet, I have cared deeply to have approval, specifically from people I respect.

When I was young I believed that if I didn't tell others about Jesus Christ and how He was their only route to salvation, it would affect their soul for all eternity. If I didn't tell them, I felt guilty. And sad. And anxious. So I had to make that clear. After all, I might be that person's only vehicle for the gospel. So in my mind – the mind of a kid who believed what she was told – their damnation would be my fault. That's a lot of pressure for a kid of any age to bear. But bear it I did. And that is where my suffering and worry began.

Belief played a huge role in my childhood. From the time I was young I heard and absorbed many ideas with which I could not quite come to terms, but which I felt compelled to believe because I was taught they were true. In fact, it was true because God said it was true. People told me God said it was true. People I *trusted* told me God said it was true. And if I didn't believe some of these fundamentals of salvation, then God would not be happy with me. I would be voluntarily rejecting Him and would have to face His judgment, in this life as well as the next.

My heart truly desired welfare for everyone – in this life and the next – and my mind wanted to be free of the terrible guilt I felt for not sharing the Good News with others. As a result, anxiety was both a cause and by-product of my interactions with others. I was anxious for the other person's welfare and soul, but I was also anxious about making a fool of myself or disrespecting someone by talking to them about my beliefs. My stomach started churning and my heart started pounding as soon as I thought that I should approach someone.

I remember one cold, dark day while I was in high school. I stood waiting for the city bus in the early morning air. A young man slightly older than me was also standing waiting for the bus. After ten minutes or so spent building up my courage, I turned to him and asked him if he had heard about Jesus or if he knew him as his personal Savior. He said he had not, so I told him that Jesus had come to save us from sin and to help us in our lives. Unlike many other people I had spoken to, this man actually smiled and seemed interested. Surprised, I continued my monologue that dark morning as the birds started to come awake to breathe life to the world. I told the man how he could be saved and I had him repeat a version of the Sinner's Prayer with me. As we boarded the bus I wished him well in his life.

Standing at a corner bus stop, that man said a prayer to invite Jesus into his life. I have wondered many times since, how he is doing, and what impact, if any, my childish and simple attempt to help had on his life. When I look back at that experience now I feel a mix of empathy for myself – I was doing what I thought was ultimately helpful to people – and embarrassment at how I might have come across to that gentleman and others I talked to similarly.

I also recall English class in my junior year of high school, and the tattered journal we were required to pass back and forth. The intention was to communicate our thoughts and responses to books and assignments and to receive our teacher's comments in return. The teacher, Mr. Mateo, was an intelligent and fun-loving guitar player prone to wearing Converse sneakers. He read several of my well-meaning explanations of Jesus' important role in improving his life, complete with descriptions of how God and Jesus had already helped me in my own life. These were important, if naïve attempts to let my light shine. Mr. Mateo always gracefully replied with his own well-thought-out answers based on his life philosophy. Although I greatly respected him and his intelligence, I still felt the urge to argue that it didn't matter how much sense his philosophy made, God had made it clear that Jesus was the *only* way to be saved, and I certainly didn't want him to go to hell. I wonder now how I – the proselytizing high-schooler with the curly hair, shy smile, and impassioned pleas – appeared to him at that time .

Knowing that God was so particular about my beliefs contributed to my demand for perfection in myself: perfection in my beliefs; perfection in my relationship with God; perfection in my interactions with others. I never felt quite close enough to God, as a result. Looking back through my journals, I see that this was a daily concern. Numerous entries from October 1990 echo this sentiment, for example: "I pray I will come closer to Jesus and that I will be able to hear his voice and that he will improve me. I want to love God a lot again. Amen."

I never felt that I loved God as much as I should. Not only was I not perfect, I was also hypercritical of my imperfections. I recently found an appalling journal entry from that time period: "God showed me that in the Bible it says, 'Anyone who says bad things about their father or mother must be put to death. Mark 7:10' I won't say anything bad about my parents anymore. Dear Jesus, please forgive me for saying rotten things about my mom and dad. Please don't let me be put to death. I love you lots. Amen." I was only a very tender ten.

At that young age I was so afraid of a God who would encourage, even mandate, that parents stone their children for misbehaving that my heart raced and my stomach tensed. I knew this New Testament verse was backed up in the Old Testament; I had read it there myself. God had told his people, the Israelites, to stone their children if they didn't obey. Wasn't the Bible *literally* true and inspired by God? And wasn't God unchanging? The people I respected told me so and I believed them, or at least struggled to believe them because I was told I should. In my soul, however, I didn't believe that if God was love He would ask something so cruel. Then I remembered the story of God commanding Abraham to offer up Isaac, to prove that he loved God more than his own son. Maybe He would require it in my case as well, I reasoned. My head started to hurt. I didn't want to chance it. I *had* to recognize my sin and ask for forgiveness, for everything.

At fourteen I wrote, "I have been truly naughty. I don't do what You want me to all the time. Jesus, right now the biggest sin I can think of is that I've been neglecting my prayer and reading of your word." That same year I wrote, "I have sinned today: not put up my suspenders when mom wanted me to, not going downstairs immediately, not watching my siblings how I should have, etc." When I was fifteen I wrote about something I figured I'd done wrong, "I love you and I'm sorry for ignoring you and hurting you like that. Please forgive me. I love you a lot! I really want to draw nearer to you. Please show me how to study the scriptures the way you want me to – thank you. I love you. Love, your daughter, servant and friend, me." Not only did I have to be perfect in my beliefs and in my behavior, I also had to make sure I didn't hurt God's feelings or upset Him, that He received enough attention in our relationship!

Intolerance

Another side effect of the understanding that people had to believe "just so," was my judgmental attitude toward others whose beliefs differed from my own. I had been taught that God required people to believe at least a few basics tenets in order to get to heaven. People who didn't believe them were thus wrong, blind, and pitiable, and ultimately saved from themselves. I see now that although I intended to be compassionate by attempting to save unbelievers, I was also condescending and patronizing, even toward grown people such as my unbelieving hippy English teacher and my Christian Scientist Social Studies teacher. I thought I knew their best interest; in reality I simply could not acknowledge their right to their own minds, beliefs, and spirituality or lack thereof.

I remember understanding, even as a schoolgirl, that my drive to save others, to convince them to believe differently, caused my peers to perceive me as a goody-goody. I realized they were uncomfortable being themselves around me. This created a dilemma for me: on the one hand, as a loving and respectful person, I wanted people to be themselves, to feel good about themselves, yet trying to change them had the opposite effect.

My high school boyfriend once wrote me a note that said, "Your level of Christianity makes me feel small and inferior." In context, he meant this as a put down on his own character and "level of Christianity." I wanted to encourage others to feel valued, cared for, whole, and respected, not inferior, self-doubting and self-flagellating, so it pained me to know that the result of my influence was self-judgment and self-doubt instead of inspiration.

It turns out I was projecting my anxiety onto others. I was so concerned with loving God in just the right way, setting the right example, and telling others how to do it right, that instead of enjoying a relationship with God and loving my "brothers and sisters," I was infecting them with the same anxiety I had about the unworthy state of their souls.

Doubt

For almost as long as I can remember, in addition to intolerance, I struggled a lot with doubt: doubt in Jesus and the character of God; doubt that He was real, that He came to earth, that He died; doubt that I had to believe in order to be saved or that I was saved at all; doubt whether He cared at all and–big breath–that He could really be mean enough to throw people into hell. I was particularly skeptical that the God of the Old Testament and the Jesus of the New

Testament seemed so different, though I'd been told they were the same. I wondered why God would condemn us if He'd actually made us and loved us. Where was the fairness in giving us free choice then condemning us for using it?

After contemplating such questions, I would then mentally flagellate myself for doubting. And so the cycle went: doubt, self-flagellation, doubt, self-flagellation, until I got so depressed and anxious about my unbelieving heart that at the age of thirteen I went downstairs to the medicine cabinet, opened a bottle of pills and peered inside. I sat there, holding the bottle in my hand, moving it back and forth silently, knowing I couldn't possibly do it, but wondering nonetheless if it was worth it.

The thought of ending my tortured state of mind was very appealing. I imagined no longer throwing myself on my bed in tears, my chest heaving as I prayed for God to please help me believe and relieve me from my doubt; no more headaches from constantly wondering why I was having such thoughts and what was wrong with me; no more embarrassment from being different from everyone around me.

In the end I put the cap back on the bottle and went upstairs to, once more, lie face down on my bed, crying and praying for God to release me from my suffering. I rationalized my doubt, telling myself that I really did believe, that it was the devil fighting hard against me. I considered the idea that I was crazy, or already condemned. Since I really didn't know if it was the former and I didn't want it to be the latter, I continued to fight that much harder against the devil and his evil.

My doubting left me feeling like a dirty traitor, someone who would be stoned or ostracized if word got around. Deeply ashamed of my own thoughts, my heavy heart throbbed with sadness and confusion. My anxious mind ricocheted between knowing it was created to think and do what made sense, and feeling it was too dangerous to risk not believing what it was told. I struggled on in silence, reading books, writing in my journal and talking to myself to alleviate the pressure and anxiety I felt everywhere in my body. Eventually I threw myself into my schoolwork, the one place I was able to reach near-perfection. I tried to keep the questions at bay, so that the headache would stay away and my stomach would not tighten into a zillion knots.

I didn't share my torments with anyone. I figured that telling someone within the church would get me nowhere and telling someone outside the church would just cement their idea of my misfit status. In a tortured state of questioning what was forbidden to question, I truly felt that the only consequence of doubt was rejection. When I was thirteen I wrote in my journal, "Lord, please help me. I'm calling out to you in desperation; I think I don't believe Christ died and was raised from the dead. Please help me to believe that and also to believe that Christ and God all exist. I'm praying this to you because I know you're the only one who can help me to believe. No one else can help the way I need you to. Lord, please help me. I'm desperate. Help!!"

Relief

As an adult, one of my biggest shifts toward relief has been to finally stop believing in hell, and I remember the exact moment I did so. I had been married for some time and was standing in the bathroom of our third home, looking down at the floor as I slowly wiped my hands on a towel. It suddenly occurred to me that I did not *have* to believe in hell. No one was making me believe in hell. Believing in hell was not serving me. I had the power to release myself. Could it be that God might not actually be angry with me if I stopped?

I had always loved and trusted God, always trusted that He would direct my steps if I paid attention. Didn't it follow that I could also trust that God made me who I was, made me with a mind that searched for knowledge, wisdom, and understanding? Wasn't it precisely my philosophical nature—my penchant for doubt; my habit of not buying in to certain beliefs; my interest in looking for proof and deeper meaning—that made me who I was? More importantly, wasn't it my discerning mind that allowed me to feel God's love and compassion rather than vindictiveness and anger? Could it be that God was finally answering my prayer to show me who He really was? Wasn't it true that when I resisted where my soul was taking me, I was resisting God himself?

I knew in that moment, with the smell of soap on my hands and the sound of the TV and my husband down the hallway, that even if my journey took me away and then back again, it was a journey I had to take. It was a journey I *wanted* to take and I was finally giving myself permission to embark. The ultimate nature of reality – including whether hell really existed or not–I would leave to God. I would trust God instead of trusting my beliefs.

The thought gave me incredible peace: the greatest freedom I had ever given myself, the greatest freedom God had ever given me. Could they be the same thing? Releasing hell meant that I could value other people's religions and journeys as well. It meant that I didn't have to try to change a butterfly into a ladybug, but could admire both and see each as uniquely created by a God who was not trying to change one into the other. On the contrary, He had made them that way in the first place!

Reflection

The result of my revelation is that I now see and appreciate life around me. I live from my soul without the fear of being responsible for everyone else. In one moment I learned to live *in* the question, rather than fighting against it. I gave up my childish need to be certain about belief and the truths of the universe. I found new value in my own unique experience, different though it was from others.

As an adult, one part of me could not believe that I had taken what I'd read and been told - about God, hell, the Bible, about anything, really - so much to heart. Another part of me remembered exactly how it felt to have such a believing heart that had served me so well growing up. I believed there was a God and that He wanted to have a relationship with me. The relationship that I built with my God was a friendship that sustained me through childhood and adolescence, through doubts and anxieties. God was my yin and my yang, there for me in all my joyful times, adventures, and big moments, supporting me in my dreams and nurturing my sense of self. I derived an enormous amount of comfort and pleasure from "knowing God" and being as loving as I could be to other people. Without such a believing nature I likely would not have forged this friendship with the God whom I was now able to see in a bigger sense than before.

Of course, for a time, I found myself very angry with my church, my parents, and the religious world at large for condoning a belief system that would or could "do that" to a little girl – or anyone– who is earnest by nature. After a few years, however, I realized that all scriptures, all teachings, all parents, and even nature itself, teach both directly and indirectly; all lessons may be misunderstood, taken out of context, and internalized, or may have unanticipated and far-reaching consequences. There are many things better taken metaphorically that some take literally and some ideas that are helpful and necessary at one time or in one culture may be unnecessary or harmful in another.

It is true that some of us come down on one side of that, some the other side, and some have no idea at all where they land. And that is okay. We do the best we can with what we have, who we are, and what we truly believe. This is exactly what my parents and church have done and ultimately what I did as well. I finally found my freedom in realizing that I don't have to struggle to make myself believe or value things that don't make sense to me. I believe life is a beautiful, perfect process with a purpose to everything that happens, even the pain and the parts we discard. Releasing myself from torturous beliefs, from anxiety about life, the afterlife, and God's character, freed me to believe that God is Love. Not only does He behave in a loving way, He is better than the best parent ever has been or ever could be.

I have given myself permission to trust my intuition about God.

Acceptance

The trouble was not that I shouldn't have wanted to help others, it's that I wasn't valuing their own journeys as legitimate. At the time, I didn't see that God had his hand on their lives as much as He had on mine. I now understand that God was influencing, guiding, loving, and holding others in the palm of His hand just as much as He was holding me. I now trust that He cares about all of our individual journeys, encouraging us onward while accepting us as-is. If change is to happen, we will be loved into it and accepted all along the way.

It is a misconception that we help people change by telling them what is wrong with them. People think and behave in ways that may or may not benefit them but that does not increase or diminish their value at all. We help them change—if they want to—by *telling them what is right with them*. By letting them know and helping them actually believe for themselves that they are loved—whether or not they cut their hair, whether or not they get a tattoo on their forehead, whether or not they believe in Jesus— we are in the best position to model positive self-growth. If they find that a way of being is not serving them, we can support them in finding out what *would* serve them and how to get there.

Instead of seeing a world that is less than perfect, I now see an intricate tapestry, a beautiful song composed by many diverse peoples, beliefs, lifestyles and ways of thinking. I think of us all as a team, each member having a different role. One traditional Christian image is that of a human body, with each person being a necessary but different part of the whole. I might be an eye, you an ear and our neighbors the kidney and spleen. If we were all eyes, ears or spleens, where would the body be? How would it function for its higher purpose? It wouldn't.

I now choose a perspective that enables me to view and relate to humanity—and myself—in a way that serves me well. I no longer insist on changing others. Rather I celebrate our differences, our similarities, our complexities, and yes, our imperfections.

I now know that as I encountered each of the personal truths revealed here, I shifted bit by bit. I let go of the old anxieties, and as I did I began sharing more positive energy with others. Each small thing said or done, thought or read in an old journal, turned my wheels just slightly—a few degrees at a time, eventually resulting in a significant direction change. No longer preaching a particular belief or value system, I now leave the business of what happens to others in God's very capable hands. I free myself to operate my life according to what I know to be true for me and I allow others to do the same. Just as God is guiding and loving me, I now believe He is interacting with everyone equally. It is up to us to notice it and respond to this interaction. I choose to notice. I choose to revel in God's presence in the universe, in every flower, every person, every song, every opportunity.

Invitation

Intolerance of ourselves and others causes so much heartache and division, the opposite of the deep peace, love, and connection that we seek. I wish for everyone, starting with you, to join me in the process of acceptance. Let go. Release yourself to embrace your own truth—the song of *your* soul—instead of what others tell you to do or believe. Release your hold on what doesn't work for you as you allow others to do the same. Close your eyes and feel the deep peace and perfection within yourself, just as you are.

It starts with you, dear reader. It starts with me. Embracing our own truth gives others the courage to do the same. Peace to you on your journey.

Questions for Reflection

- What are you not accepting about yourself? About others? How would it benefit you to move into acceptance?

- How would your life be enhanced if you allowed yourself to be who you are instead of who you think you should be?

- What about my story resonates for you in your own journey? What does not resonate? What does this mean for you?

- How might you make use of this information in your own life?

About Abigail Bruce

Abigail Bruce, PHR, CPC, ACC, is a Certified Whole Person Coach through the Baraka Institute, and has coached people from many different walks of life. She is currently an employee relations specialist with FedEx Ground and spends much of her time coaching internal employees, in addition to seeing external clients. Her niche areas are Work/Life Balance, Leadership, and Spirituality.

Abigail has additional experience teaching and tutoring math and English as a Second Language to diverse immigrant groups and study abroad students. She has studied and lived in Russia, and enjoys learning the Russian language. Her other creative outlets include singing, painting, piano, photography, knitting, reading, writing, hiking, and playing with her son and husband.

Abigail is on a continuing journey of learning and experimentation with various spiritual thoughts and practices. She has served her church through singing and leadership for the past seventeen years. She continually finds herself contemplating life, the nature of reality, and the individual expression of spirituality.

www.abigailbruce.com

from the end to the beginning

SELF TRANSFORMATION AFTER BRAIN SURGERY
by Ben Luskin

There comes a time in everyone's life when he or she reflects back to ask, "How? How did I get from where I was then to where I am today?"

On September 28, 1994, on a four-lane highway on the coast of Lake Superior, the minivan I was riding in was hit by a semi-truck traveling at high speed. Seated in the back driver's-side corner, I took the brunt of the impact. Fortunately, I was wearing my seat belt, which prevented me from flying forward through the windshield, but the jolt I received smashed my brain into my skull, spinning me into a coma. I was 12 years old at the time.

Lying there, gasping for breath, with nothing but my vital signs intact, my future looked grim. Just then, an off-duty ER nurse came rolling down the same stretch of backwoods highway. He pulled over, cleared my airway, and called for an ambulance. The ambulance soon arrived and transported me to the Cook County North Shore Hospital, a small emergency facility in Grand Marais, Minnesota. There they inserted a tube down my throat into my lungs to stabilize my breathing before transporting me via helicopter to the nearest intensive care unit at St. Luke's Hospital in Duluth. I spent two weeks at St. Luke's, during which they put a tracheotomy tube in my throat for breathing, a tube in my nose for eating, and a urinary catheter in my bladder.

Once I was well enough, I was taken to Gillette Children's Hospital in St. Paul, Minnesota. I spent the next six weeks unconscious, before I started to come to.

At first I could only remember a few seconds at a time, then minutes, then hours. Once I could remember coherent sequences, I struggled with chronological order. I would remember something that happened to me the previous night as if it happened five minutes ago.

I felt weak and vulnerable during this time; not sure if I was living in a dream or reality, everything seemed surreal. Like a child confronted by shadows in the dark, I looked to my mother for comfort, requesting that she make me a tape of lullabies. Not at all confident with her voice, she overcame her doubts and recorded herself singing. "Anything for my son," she would later say. I remember listening to that tape over and over again in my hospital bed. It occupied a place in my heart next to Metallica's *Master of Puppets*.

Meanwhile, I began to notice myself regaining lost skills on a daily basis. Beginning with gross movements, and then finer gestures, my body gradually shook back into action. While I don't remember which movements came first, I can clearly recall the excitement that accompanied the first time I was able to clench and unclench my fist. Eventually I was able to leave my bed and hobble around my room with the assistance of a walker, meander down the hall, or to the cafeteria for a snack.

Taken in perspective, my path of development was similar to that of an infant growing into a toddler. I went from being bed-ridden monitored every minute, to cruising gradually longer distances. Then, just as there is a point in a child's life when he must say good bye to everlasting free time and enter school, there came a point when I had to say good bye to my open days of roaming and begin a rigid routine of rehabilitation.

In place of reading, writing, and math classes, my regime consisted of different forms of rehab. I had physical, occupational, speech, recreational therapy, and more, one after the other, from morning until afternoon. I remember various lessons from each. There were those days in PT spent relearning how to walk, with my therapist holding an elastic band around my leg to provide resistance. And there were those days in OT when I played catch with a Velcro ball. In speech therapy I played computer games, like *Where in the World is Carmen Sandiego*, and in recreational therapy I built crude objects out of brightly colored blocks. These therapies helped me to regain basic skills.

I continued my academic education during this time as well. I remember both my mom and dad spending hours at my bedside working to catch me up on everything I was missing in the first half of seventh grade. My friends, too, helped to catch me up by reading chapter books aloud.

There were also empty times in my schedule, which, like many of my peers, I filled with watching TV in bed. Some of my favorite movies were Disney's *Robin Hood* and Sylvester Stallone's *Cliffhanger*. My favorite show was *Married with Children*. Al Bundy really did it for me, which says a little about my sense of humor at the time. I used to laugh this really annoying laugh, exhaling silently and then inhaling, sounding like a sick seagull.

It didn't take much to get a rise out of me during this time. With a poor gauge of what speech and behavior were appropriate, I acted more-or-less without a conscience. I found crude jokes absolutely hilarious and poured affection on those hospital visitors and staff who were able to deliver these inappropriate gems. In general, any joke with a four-letter word would do the trick.

I tried my hand in the comedy trade as well. Considering my state of health at the time, seldom did anyone step in to correct me. Thus the only real feedback I got was my own--the louder I laughed, the funnier my jokes were. It wasn't until I went back to middle school, where my jokes were subjected to the scrutiny of my peers that I realized not everyone was laughing.

Home visits came next. Starting with simple day trips and then stretching into weekend stays, these excursions served two purposes: they brought me back to what my life had been and helped prepare me for what my life was to become. My first trip home was around Halloween. I remember demanding to bring a mask and costume back to the hospital with me for trick-or-treating. I also remember vividly the drives up and down the parking ramp of the hospital. The twists and turns gave me a killer headache.

And then the big day came. The caring staff cut my bracelet, hugging me as we said our goodbyes. That was it. I was no longer a patient, but a member of the greater community. After three long months spent behind those hospital doors, I felt like a long-term inmate. I knew the rundown of the place. I could get you a cup of orange juice, a deck of playing cards, or an extra blanket for your bed. Now I was out!

In the following years, I passed through five successive stages of development: denial, acceptance, rejection, balance, and transformation.

Immediately following my release from the hospital, I entered the first stage: denial. Like other kids my age, I could not see beyond the surface reality of pleasure and pain. Happiness was but a sensual and immediate experience to me, so it was to this end that I invested my energy. I was often unaware of the inappropriateness of my actions and soon gained a reputation for off-kilter behavior. Nevertheless, I didn't think much of my injury or its effects during this period, which took up the totality of my high school career. I just went ahead and lived my life, enjoying friends, music, Boy Scouts, psychedelics, reading, writing, and other activities.

Although I didn't think much about my injury, it impacted me in profound ways. Striking closest to home, my relationship with my sister suffered greatly. Because I could no longer keep up with her grades and other accomplishments, I convinced myself that hard work was a waste of time. I withdrew from many of the activities I had been involved in before the accident, putting less effort into learning to play trumpet and challenging myself less academically, taking the easiest courses that I could get away with.

I was also very sensitive during this time. It did not take much for me to explode in anger, throw up my hands, and stomp away. Often furious at my parents, I responded to many of their requests by hurling obscenities and locking myself in my room. I also remember wanting to change schools because I was mad at my friends. A few times I even stomped out of school.

The effects of my injury came out most through my constant mumbling. As a result, my friends routinely took advantage of me. I could list a slew of cruel pranks even my best friends pulled on me, but I'd rather not. I don't hold this against them. They were in the midst of their own stages of development.

My lack of independence was another major hindrance. Even when I could manage by myself, I impulsively asked others for help. A task as simple as determining where to plug in the vacuum cleaner, for example, seemed somehow impossible to me. I would try half-heartedly to figure out a way around such obstacles before getting frustrated and looking to others for guidance.

Predictably, few girls wanted anything to do with me, a seemingly helpless gimp. I could put on a good show, but once I left the stage, I couldn't hang. I never knew what to say or how to act. And when I did express myself, it was usually through colorful expressions too off-the-wall for most girls to appreciate. Still, my high school career was not devoid of female attention. I did find a few girls--mostly at rave parties--nearly as crazy as me.

I graduated with a good GPA so I applied and was admitted to Lewis and Clark College, a private liberal arts school in Portland, Oregon. Leaving everything familiar behind in Minneapolis to begin a new life as a college student, I felt like an immigrant in a new land. Surrounded by foreign customs, language, and weather patterns, my life on campus presented numerous challenges and my limitations quickly came to the forefront. I struggled to keep up my hygiene, social life, and general sense of confidence.

I also found myself engrossed in new ideas and beliefs. And so it was that I became intrigued by the ancient Chinese philosophy of the *Tao*, or "The Way," and spent many hours sitting in the tall grasses of a nearby ravine contemplating its meaning. As a result, I slowly began to accept my lot and just "go with the flow." It was then that I entered the second stage of my development: acceptance.

In this new stage, I acknowledged my limitations and worked around them, focusing my efforts on intellectual pursuits and self-discovery. I became a hermit, reading books by candlelight late into the evening. Consequently, college became a worthwhile venture, fulfilling and entertaining. I put less effort into socializing and more into learning, and graduated with a Bachelor of Arts in Religious Studies.

After graduation, not much changed at first. Most of my good friends hung around Portland, and we did as we'd always done. As the summer started to slip away, I began thinking about what I was going to do next. When it came time to make a decision, I complied with what my family thought was best for me--working a secure job with benefits. I found employment with the Portland Public Schools where I worked as a para-educator for two years.

At this job many of the same issues--my vulnerability, lack of independence, and so forth--continued to get in my way. Discerning what was expected of me proved exceedingly difficult, and my superiors regularly reprimanded me for taking too much initiative. Had it not been for the unwavering support of my friends, I'm not sure I would have survived this episode as well as I did. Then, about half-way through my second year working for the school district, two things happened that would drastically change the course of my life: I discovered martial arts, and I met a woman.

I met Mary on a flight from Minneapolis back to Portland the day before New Year's Eve, 2005. Content with my visit back to my spawning grounds, and eager to return to the independent life I had crafted for myself, I stepped confidently onto the plane and took a seat. Just then, a beautiful woman asked if she could squeeze by into the seat next to mine. And that's when the magic began.

Carrying on meaningful conversations had long been a struggle for me, with my poor tact and worse timing. To compensate, I had taken up residence in that space between seriousness and ridiculousness. My good friends knew me well and understood that I coated 99.9 percent of what I said and did with a thick layer of irony and facetiousness. They also knew there was often a kernel of truth buried underneath. As a result, conversations with strangers were a great challenge. More often than not, I'd get the polite head-bob followed by the walk-away.

But this beautiful lady sat down next to me with nowhere to go for a three full hours. I grinned and wondered, "Is this a golden opportunity or what?" From there things just kept getting better. As it turned out, she was a student of Chinese medicine, and therefore quite familiar with the philosophy of the Tao that had so influenced my own life. By the time the plane landed, we had arranged to spend the following evening, New Year's Eve, together.

After a short period of courting, we had fallen head-over-heels for each other. Despite all the dissimilarities in our lifestyles and aspirations—an 11-year age difference, her desire to have a family and settle down, my youthful hunger for adventure—we were convinced that we were meant for each other. Ignoring all the little voices in our heads, we went on singing and dancing, and before long had a baby on the way.

Before a man becomes a father, he spends a good number of months knowing he will become a father. In addition to my personal struggles concerning social interactions, gainful employment, and basic survival skills, to name just a few, I now had to face the fact that I would ultimately be responsible for the life of another being, my child. There was no turning back.

I freaked out. My life began to unravel before my eyes. This was neither what I had asked for, nor what I had prepared to do. With my aspirations for post-grad adventures thrown out the window, my eagerly anticipated quest for adventure became little more than a passing fancy. My fate, I realized, had already been determined, and I had eight months to buck up for the ride.

So I did what most would do in that kind of situation. I hung my head and moped. I don't know how the next step came to be. Perhaps the way my head drooped pulled me in a particular direction. Perhaps there was some force in the universe looking out for me. Suffice it to say, one of my melancholy walks led me straight through the doors of a martial arts studio. Those doors would provide opportunities greater than I had ever dreamed.

From the get-go, martial arts gave me a reason to focus on potential and growth rather than limitations and stagnancy. Martial arts also did much to prepare me for the responsibilities and roles that I was soon to assume, helping me to understand the pleasures derived from hard work and dedication. With this mindset, I entered the delivery room.

While stories of instant love and attachment are popular among new parents, this is not at all what happened to me. Rather, I spent the first several months of Avi's life emerging from a state of fear-induced paralysis. During this time, it was not so much love that inspired me to keep going, as it was a sense of duty. All things considered, those months were a great awakening for me, a time to reassess the value of various influences in my life. I owe much gratitude to Mary for her unwavering support throughout.

So there I was, a new father with a little baby girl looking to me to make the world cozy for her. In addition, I was training regularly and developing confidence and ability at a break-neck pace. Considering these two circumstances, I realized that in order to manifest a desired reality, I needed to stop dealing with my life as it unfolded. It was time for me to take control. Then and there I entered the next stage of my development: rejection.

This epiphany set off a chain of events that changed the very foundations of my life. With strong determination directing every move, I quit my job, moved to Eugene--a small, part university/part blue-collar city two hours from Portland--and entered the world of manual labor. This was a drastic move for me, considering that I had no experience with physical labor, save for mowing a lawn or two. I came from an intellectual family and had spent my childhood focused on intellectual pursuits. Everyone who knew me thought what I was doing was foolish, and they told me so.

No matter. I'd led myself to believe I was in control. I threw myself into my new lifestyle with fervor and for a brief time was content with the new identity I had forged for myself. I came to devalue intellectual pursuits and academic knowledge. I worked hard and lived an honest and simple life, returning home each day, exhausted and filthy, to a loving partner and a cooing baby daughter.

After several months, this pleasant existence fell prey to the harsh facts of reality. Unable to perform sufficiently, I lost job after job, and soon sank into a dark place of discouragement, depression, and self-pity. I spent entire days in bed, convinced that I would never be good at anything worthwhile; all I had going for me was the fact that I was a "good person." In the words of Richard Farina, I'd "been down so long it looked like up to me." I had become so frustrated with my life that I began to crave despair. I refused all help from others, preferring torment to relief, until one day I grudgingly accepted help from a job coach, who helped me to find work at Lane Community College supporting adults with developmental disabilities.

This job turned out to be my ticket to the fourth stage of my development: balance. What began as a simple means to make ends meet soon became a waterfall of opportunity. For the first time in my life, I discovered that my skills were perfect for the work expected of me. Having grown up with a brother on the autism spectrum, and having worked in the field of special education for many years, developmental disabilities were nothing new to me. As I gained confidence and earned my co-workers' respect, my limitations disappeared.

From that point on, I determined to perform at my highest level, to accomplish more than I had previously considered possible. Feeling for the first time in a long while that I had things under control,

I transferred the focus of my thoughts from personal survival to affecting positive change on a broad scale. I began brainstorming ideas concerning how to benefit my clients' lives. My superiors encouraged me to follow through with these ideas; before long I had implemented a non-combative martial arts training program for my clients. My next move was to draft and edit a program newsletter, *News from Next Door*, which provided clients with opportunities to share their extracurricular interests and pursuits.

I was gaining momentum and nothing less than a granite wall could stop my ascent. Ideas seemed to flow through my brain from the moment I woke up until the moment I fell asleep. I'm sometimes amazed at how it all happened, as though a force greater than myself held the steering wheel. And so it was that I woke up one cloudy autumn day and realized that I had devised a new strategy for rehabilitation and written an extensive paper on its design.

My next step was to begin offering my services to others. I launched a rehabilitation business out of my garage, volunteered time with various organizations, and taught workshops wherever and whenever I could. I now had something to be proud of, a skill to share with others.

By this time my dedication to martial arts and its principles had become one of my strongest foundations. Self-discipline, responsibility, and compassion had become my most valued traits. I trained regularly with an instructor, and when I wasn't training formally, I conditioned my body and mind through various exercises and activities. As a result, the profound gifts I received from martial arts flowed unrestrained into my work. The strength that I felt in the dojo was matched by the strength I felt while assisting others in overcoming their challenges.

Like a June flower with ample water and sunshine, my stem grew stronger and my colors brighter. I searched far and wide for opportunities to share my work with others, spurred on by my passion and a belief that success was inevitable. I found that audiences tended to receive my message well. Though I also experienced setbacks, each one taught me a new lesson about myself in relation to the universe. Over all, my very understanding of the duality of good and bad, right and wrong, was overturned. My characteristic skepticism and doubt was put in check. I was transformed into a new person, one congruent with his deepest values and beliefs.

Next I acquired professional certification as a Life Coach through the Baraka Institute in Portland. With credentials in my pocket, I stepped up my game and boldly set forth to pave a new trail in the professional world. I said goodbye to my friends and colleagues at the community college and established a private practice, Launch Empowerment Mentoring, under which I continued to serve clients, teach workshops, and advocate for positive change in the field of mental health. Having finally found comfort underneath my skin, I entered the fifth stage: transformation.

Today, with the confidence and resources to become whoever and whatever I wish, I have again turned inward, hoping to find within myself the keys to success. Just as in college, I spend much of my time alone, reading, writing, training, and thinking. I hold myself to the strictest of routines, waking up early to run through a number of exercises before beginning each day. In the community I pour my efforts into networking and various empowerment-themed projects. In the presence of my children (Mary and I are still together raising two beautiful daughters) I work to hold myself with strength and confidence, embodying the qualities I believe most valuable.

While experiencing this great transformation within myself, I've observed the efforts I've poured into the community beginning to pay off. I notice friends and strangers alike receiving me in a more dignified way, regarding me with admiration. Perhaps most rewarding, I find others turning to me for support.

What lies around the next bend is uncertain, and I like it that way. This uncertainty gives me confidence that what happens next is exactly what needs to happen. What I do know is that if I work hard and stay true to my values, my life will be endowed with countless gifts. So I spend my days strengthening my mind, body, and spirit in order that I may benefit others--my family, friends, neighbors, students, and teachers--to the greatest of my ability.

As I close this chapter, I encourage you to consider the challenges that you've faced in your own life. Whether as serious as a Traumatic Brain Injury or not, the lessons they offer can be just as valuable.

Questions for Reflection

- What do your current and past challenges teach you about yourself?

- How did they affect you yesterday?

- How do they affect you today?

- And most importantly, how can they help you to realize your potential?

About Ben Luskin

Ben Luskin, CPC is a Certified Whole Person Coach, author, and voice for empowerment in Eugene, Oregon. He is the founder and director of Launch Empowerment Mentoring, a support service specializing in assisting and empowering individuals living with brain injuries, mental health, and cognitive challenges.

Following a life spent in recovery from a traumatic brain injury, Ben has become convinced that all individuals hold within themselves the tools they need to succeed. He encourages shifts in perception to help his clients find strength to accept their current situations and focus on development. Along with his work, Ben trains in the martial art of Sun Moo Do under Grandmaster Bong Pil Yang. He shares life with his loving partner, Mary, and their two beautiful daughters, Avi and Pearl.

www.launchmentor.com

ONE *New* THING

by Danea Horn

Get up, let the dogs out, work, eat lunch, work, let the dogs out, feed the dogs, eat dinner, watch TV. My rut was fully solidified. I would have fits-and-starts of newness—new workout tape, new breakfast cereal— but the pattern was essentially unchanged. My comfort zone was nice and cozy, complete with an indent on my side of the couch.

Life was about familiarity, comfort, and avoidance. I had dreams but came up with lots of excuses about why now was never quite the right time to pursue them. Each time I turned on the television, I was ignoring my thoughts, drowning them out with the laugh tracks and drama. I lived in a world of the characters' story lines so that I didn't have to think about how I was living my own.

From the outside, my life appeared picturesque. I owned a home, made a great salary, received promotions and praise, and I was married to a man who was amazing in too many ways to count...but I couldn't take any of it in. Logically, I could see the success, but the feeling was just not there. I longed for a career I was passionate about; I dreamed of coaching and speaking and writing. I wanted to wake up and feel grateful. All I felt was stuck and burdened, a woman going through the motions but not making any real progress.

Sure, I read all the self-help books, and I mean *all* the books. I made lists of goals, I looked at my limiting beliefs, visited my inner child, analyzed values and created affirmations, but again, each evening when I got home, I followed the same routine, never putting my dreams into action. My mind claimed to be on board with wanting change, but I could not find enough drive to make that change happen. I did not want to look back on my life and say that I watched every episode of *Friends* three times, but never got around to taking action to write a book or become a coach. Dinner always had to be made, there was a television show I couldn't miss, the dogs needed walking and well, "I had a hard day at work and deserve a rest."

The Television Pastime

There is a funny thing about television. We use it as a relaxation tool, but very seldom is it actually relaxing. Think about it: you sit down to "just watch this one 30-minute show," and before you know it, three hours have gone by while you have drained yourself of all motivation and forgotten what was on your to-do list.

Our brains operate in one of five different brain wave frequencies at any given time. They are listed below in order of the quickest- to the slowest-moving frequencies:

- **Gamma**: High focus and awareness.
- **Beta**: Normal functioning level.
- **Alpha**: Relaxed state — more open to subconscious suggestion.
- **Theta**: Extremely relaxed — associated with dreaming and imagining; also very receptive to unconscious suggestion.
- **Delta**: Deep sleep.

The alpha brain wave frequency is the best state to be in when using positive self-talk because your unconscious mind is more open to suggestion. Unfortunately, this is also the same state you are in when you watch TV. Studies have shown that watching TV puts you into an alpha brain wave state within the first minute of watching[1]. This means that your energy level is low, and that you are extremely receptive to

---

[1] Krugman, H.E. "The Impact of Television Advertising: Learning Without Involvement," Public Opinion Quarterly, Vol. 29, No. 3. (1965)

the messages coming across the screen. Receptive to shows such as *CSI*, *I Am Pregnant and In Prison* (yes, this really is a reality show), *Jersey Shore*, *The Apprentice*, *The Hills*, and any other ridiculousness you subject your mind to. It also means that you are receptive to the numerous commercials shown; advertisers love this about TV.

When I was watching TV, I was actually opening my mind to ideas that were not restorative or empowering. I wasn't feeling rejuvenated after a long day at work, only sucked in and even more tired.

The Question

After years of the same-old-same-old I had a coach ask me, "What do you want?" I could have said a number of things: "I want to be an author"; "I want to speak in front of audiences"; "I want to be a life coach"; "I want more money." I had the lists, I knew what my goals were, but what came out of my mouth was so authentic and surprising, it brought me to tears: "I want to dance."

Let's back up for a moment. Dance used to be a big part of my life. At age four, I started in ballet, which led to jazz, high school drill team, and cheerleading. If I was stressed in college, I would shut the dorm room door and turn up the music while I wildly flailed about. At Christmas each year, I would do a living room performance of my one-woman rendition of *The Nutcracker* while my husband, Phillip, sits dutifully as my one-man audience. In my late 20s, I was taking a jazz dance class and one day, while harnessing my inner antelope and leaping across the floor, I landed on the side of my foot and tore my knee's anterior cruciate ligament. After that injury I was too nervous to dance. I thought that giving up dance would not be a big deal, but something inside of me really missed the presence and joy that dancing creates.

When I dance, I get lost in the music—I feel alive. So while saying, "I want to dance" did mean that I would be interested in testing out my knee and joining a local dance class, it was much more than that. I was saying that "I want to engage with life." Dance was my way to fully express my essence, to feel "in the flow" and connected to something greater than myself.

The phrase "engage with life" has a different meaning for everyone. It is a way of saying that you want to live from a place of possibility. The idea of *living* in possibility was at odds with what I had been doing in all of my self-help searching. I was only contemplating possibility; I was not living it. Living it requires action and taking action meant getting out of my introspective comfort zone to do something, *anything*.

The first thing to do? Turn off the TV. I committed to that. The same evening that the coach asked me what I wanted was the last night I watched TV for six months. The second thing I did was dance. My knee injury had healed long ago and I knew that with caution I could take it for a test drive.

Friday evening of that same week, I decided to take a salsa dancing class. I had never salsa danced before. On such short notice, I would be taking the class alone. I put on my orange twirly skirt and black strappy sandals and headed for the Latin club. The group class was going to begin at nine o'clock but I arrived ten minutes early to an empty club. I found a chair fit for the high school wallflower I was quickly melting into as I reminded myself that maybe this test of vulnerability would aid in my quest to "engage with life."

Nine o'clock and a few couples had arrived, but no class yet. During the next painstaking 30 minutes, I became utterly embarrassed as more people began crowding in around me— the fact that I was alone becoming more obvious by the minute. When would that class start? Finally, at 9:30, class began. One of the most terrifying moments in life is being a single at a couples dance class. The instructor asked a few of the club regulars to assist the three single women searching wide-eyed for a partner and hoping to minimize the time spent standing alone. I danced with the instructor. Class went smoothly, and being twirled about to the Latin rhythms made my heart flutter. Just when I thought it had started, class was over. We had been taught the basic steps and one spin, it was now time for open dancing.

I thanked the instructor and stealthily retreated to my wallflower seat as I watched the floor pile up with talented dancers for whom this was obviously not the first time. Their hips could tell numerous stories of steamy salsa nights. With the grace of a saint, a young gentleman asked me to dance. He had no idea what he was in for. I bumped into him and stepped on my own toe within the first eight bars of music. He was a champ and brought it back to beginner level as the music played on. In total, three Latin masters were kind enough to dance with me that evening. I was scared, mortified, and exhilarated all at the same time. When I got home, I was intoxicated by dancing – I turned on the music, and created a one-woman salsa after-party and the next morning hatched a plan.

One New Thing

I was thrilled to have a taste for what engaging with life meant. In a salsa club, despite my trepidation, I had lived from a place of possibility, and I wanted more. The plan was simple: try one new thing each week. My logical mind knew that if I had just made a resolution to "try new things," I would never actually commit to seeking out new experiences. I needed a deadline. By Sunday of each week, I had to have tried one new thing.

First was salsa dancing. Second was tango. This time I convinced my hubby to join me. (As a side note, trying new things with your partner is an amazing way to light a spark in a routine relationship. Statistically proven and personally tested.)

Other highlights from my plan included Nia dancing (a free-form style of dance that combines martial arts, dance technique, and the healing arts), taking a class at the bookstore, introducing myself to a stranger, taking a solo trip to the coast, and a personal favorite: the alpaca farm. I completely adore those Dr. Seuss-like animals. One of my wildest dreams is to own an alpaca farm. After a quick internet search for alpaca farms in my area, I contacted an extremely friendly couple who opened up their home and herd to me. They taught me all about caring for and the personality of alpacas. I got to pet them and take pictures. We lounged together in their pen while I watched the young ones frolic. Without this "try something new" challenge I never would have contacted strangers to visit their home. This new experience changed my mindset and fear became less of an obstacle.

My "one new thing" plan started at the beginning of the summer and ended in early fall with one last new thing: an improvisational class. You've seen the show *Whose Line Is It Anyway?* Let me tell you, those guys are t.a.l.e.n.t.e.d. Their minds work in a humanly unnatural way.

The instructor and improv veteran, Chris, taught us about character, story, and how to thoroughly make fools out of ourselves. I mastered his third lesson beautifully.

There was the "game" where you have to create ten characters in one minute: Jamaican, aristocrat, old, young, ummm…ummm, pissed-off, sad, ummm…ummm, nerd, beauty queen, Hawaiian, er….uh, slightly different (and becoming real) version of pissed-off. We also played "character telephone," where one student created a character and headed toward another person in the group who then took on the character and headed toward someone else, morphing the original creation into something that ended up sounding like Frankenstein's monster doing an impression of Shirley Temple. We created scenes about golden-egg-laying ducks, pb&j-eating bears, superhero funerals, and Simon Cowell on *The Dating Game* (my British accent sounds oddly Indian).

Through six weekly classes of embarrassment, humility, and quick thinking, I learned that being honest with yourself and with a crowd is the only way to truly evoke a laugh. It turns out honesty isn't just the key to laughter; it is also the starting point from which all change occurs. This leads me back to my concurrent challenge of living without TV.

Purposeless Silence

Clearing my plate of TV also allowed something new in: silence. Not just any kind of silence, but silence without a purpose. To understand silence without a purpose, first you have to understand silence with a purpose, commonly known as meditation. When silence is supposed to lead to enlightenment, unbridled joy, or crystal-clear clarity, that silence has a certain pressure attached to it that permeates the silence with thoughts of, "Am I doing this right?", "Why am I not feeling something?", and "Am I enlightened yet?" With this practice comes an inherent dishonesty about our starting point. It is a continual push to hope we are something or can do something that we are not or cannot yet do. In this meditative silence there is very little listening and lots of head chatter. However, silence without a purpose brings honesty to the forefront. There is no TV to drown out your inner voice, there is no pressure, there are no judgmental thoughts— all you have left is your natural state of being. Which, to be honest, is uncomfortable.

There is the subtle—or not so subtle—tugging to turn something on, an inner resistance to actually hearing what you, the real you, honestly has to say about your life. The first week is brutal. Without TV, I found myself searching out other distractions, namely cleaning and organizing. Finally, around week three, I gave in to the "sit-and-stare" during the evening and on weekends. I would spend hours sitting in our sun room staring out at the back yard. I began to be comfortable with the simplicity of my own company. With no purpose, there was no struggle. I could just sit because that was all there was to do. I wasn't trying to figure anything out or plan for my future or find my purpose. I just sat and let all of the distractions fall away.

The Challenge

Eventually, the hustle and bustle of life returned, but I was no longer afraid of the silence. I didn't feel the need for distraction, which transformed my relationship with the TV altogether. I could go back to enjoying some TV entertainment without feeling held back.

It is hard to become fulfilled if at each moment of the day you analyze your level of fulfillment without taking action to change. As the Chinese proverb goes, "Talk doesn't cook rice." That means getting out of your head and into your life. Action is an essential component of fulfillment—action through trying new things, or even action through purposeless silence. The more introspective we become, the more self-help books we read, the more we make lists of goals, look at our limiting beliefs, visit our inner children, analyze values, and create affirmations without acting on any of it, the more we focus on what is wrong and further disengage with life. This causes mopey feelings that crave sinfully delicious desserts and hours of *Real Housewives* reruns.

Grace yourself with a rest from the rut and try something new. Even if your "new thing" isn't connected to your purpose or moving your goals forward, it will be reintroducing you to life. That splendid feeling of actually, consciously being alive is not to be missed.

Questions for Reflection

- Describe what engaging with life looks like for you.

- What is one "new thing" that you have always wanted to try that you will do this week?

- What do you need to let go of to allow purposeless silence in? When will you let it go?

About Danea Horn

Danea Horn, CPC started life destined to ask big questions. After being diagnosed with a rare birth disorder, enduring numerous reconstructive surgeries, and managing chronic disease for all of her life, Danea has had to continually redefine what "being positive" means. In her view, it has very little to do with "just looking on the bright side of life." It is much more about being present with truth and letting our experiences become catalysts for growth.

Danea the creator of the popular Web site CreativeAffirmations.com has written articles for or been featured in Goodness Magazine, RenaLife magazine, GirlsOnTheGrid.com, CrazySexyLife.com, Monty'sCorner.com, and PortlandOnFire.com. Her client list includes The Tiffany & Co. Unit of Mary Kay, the Portland Trail Blazers, and the Entrepreneurs' Organization. She is the author of the upcoming book *The Positivity Prescription: Rewriting the Rules for Coping with Life-Altering Illness*. As a Certified Whole Person Coach and professional speaker, Danea works with people to find their own definition of positivity, and helps them to move toward a fulfilling and productive life despite challenges.

www.DaneaHorn.com

the Kiss

by Feroshia Knight

In any given relationship, the depth of "experience" that each person perceives they are sharing with the other has always puzzled me. My mother, for example, had little time to truly experience my father before he left her. Despite his ever-expanding libido and rumored harem, this man with brilliant red hair and thick glasses was at the center of her heart.

Of course, it was the Sixties, the era of free love. Sex was its own reward. *Was she so blinded by love?* In the few years they were together, she worked numerous jobs and sacrificed her own education to support his medical career as his devoted wife.

My parents' marriage lasted barely long enough to produce me, and for that I am forever grateful. Yet I still have questions. Clearly their experience of one another was on different levels. Did my father love my mother? Did he want, understand, or even enjoy their adventure? Was it true that his own mother offered to help him with medical school if he left before my birth? After all, he was there and gone in less time than it took to say *"In-A-Gadda-Da-Vida."*

Though I have no recollection of my father, I want to believe that

I've done a thorough job accurately experiencing the other people in my life. But I acknowledge that may not be entirely true of everyone with whom I have shared myself. Sometimes we just don't allow ourselves to get close enough to see the real person beneath the skin. Skippy was one of those people.

In junior high, Skippy was the guy my girlfriends and I sneered at, looking down our noses, while murmuring, "Nice guy maybe for you, but definitely not for me. Not now, *not ever!*" You know this boy. He's the awkward one; socially inept, especially with females that you are certain he'll never experience or be experienced by any girl—*especially you.*

At the risk of being unkind, from my pre-teen perspective, Skippy, aka "Four Eyes," had well-earned his geek status. He wore inch-thick glasses and sprouted a crop of inflamed pimples, enlarged and positively glowing, apparently ripe for the picking. He had a pip-squeak voice, crooked picket-fence teeth, and a doughy belly that jiggled as he awkwardly walked the school hallways. What's more, he had side-swept his greasy strawberry hair to perfection—perfection for a nerd, that is. Although he was a smart kid and his magnificent jaw line reminded me of Superman, the sum total of his social package sabotaged him from every angle.

Despite the fact that we never really talked, Skippy had a crush on me.

I too was a brainiac with strawberry-blonde hair and crooked teeth. But I was adamant that our similarities ended there. My chic style, prominently featuring a Farrah Fawcett "do" and Calvin Klein jeans, bolstered the tenuous belief that I was everything Skippy was not. Besides, I didn't wear glasses and my zit count topped out at two. Of course, *my* zits were strategically placed: one just inside my nose (out of view, but plenty painful) and one smack dab in the middle of my forehead like a neon Hindu bindi, large, obtrusive, and visible for miles. If I were honest, each character flaw I shared with Skippy was just another reason to disdain him.

In 1978, I was thirteen. My morning routine consisted of brushing my teeth and hair, washing my face, popping my zits, donning one of my gaudy shirts sparkling with glitter and of course, jumping into those Calvins. I was obsessed with silver and gold threads and satin fabrics. To most in my age group, I'm sure my disco wear seemed weird. Maybe that was one of the reasons I was occasionally bullied. I had been chased, thrown on the ground, and humiliated more than once. To further complicate this vital time in my intellectual and emotional growth, my body danced back and forth between toothpick-thin and pillowy. My mother had implanted the idea that only thin girls are attractive, and the society in which I lived reinforced that concept exceedingly well.

As background to my morning routine, I listened to the radio or various 8-tracks, including the Bee Gees, Captain & Tenille, Barry Manilow, Glen Campbell, and John Denver. I would then gulp down breakfast (slipping as much as possible to the dog), dash to school, find my seat, and prepare to raise my hand for the teacher's questions. I was a good student and happy to be recognized as the ostentatious girl with all the answers. "Weird" aptly described me and, over time, I adopted the word to embrace my uniqueness. My deep need to be different was trumped only by my deeper need to fit in.

I became part of a pack known as the Blue Coven. Including me, there were six girls in the club. We imagined ourselves as modern witches, hoping we could have anything we wanted through the casting of magic spells. *Anything*, including Shaun Cassidy, Leif Garrett, Mark Hamill, and our own school rock stars: Mark and Jeff—but definitely *not* Skippy.

Jenny, our stern 14-year-old leader, defined two rules for the Blue Coven: First, if you agreed Jenny was the most popular girl, you were in the club; Second, if you stated or acted in any way that indicated otherwise, you were out. Jenny's boyfriend Jeff made sure of that. They were twin tyrants.

As our so-called coven formed, Jenny designed rituals to "prove our womanhood," including things like stealing our mother's pantyhose for Jenny's special date with Jeff. The rituals all fit under the umbrella of "getting noticed by boys" and we coven members carried out Jenny's orders to prove that we belonged. Whether we succeeded or failed, Jenny remained our revered Queen of Spells.

As a devotee of the coven and of love, it seemed only a matter of time until the day one of our made-up spells would really work and I would no longer be the comprehensive virgin: the last one to have kissed, sucked, slurped, touched, felt, tickled, or triumphed in any of a number of conceivable ways one could get to second base with another human being on the planet. I was determined that my status as the Virgin of Everything was going to change, so help me God! Though hopeful, I couldn't imagine when it would actually happen – especially with the extremely protective nature of my mother interfering.

The eve of our school dance arrived with the scandalizing news that Queen Jenny had been grounded after getting caught smoking. Her noticeable absence from the festivities sent shock waves throughout the seventh grade and ignited a series of events that would shape my outlook on men, relationships, *and* myself.

Jeff suspected that one of Jenny's friends had narked her out to her parents and thus ruined all the fun he'd expected to have with her. So after the dance, while huddling us together on the playing field, he directed his most wrathful suspicion at me. Jeff believed that since I was the Virgin of Everything, I must have been jealous and tattled to Jenny's parents about her vampiristic method of sucking all the smoke out of her cigarettes. While I did enjoy watching Jenny get what was coming to her, I was not the diabolical mastermind of a plan to keep her from the dance. But Jeff had command of our group and despite my pleas, the group voted, seven to none, to convict me. They decided that I must pay penance by kissing a particular boy. That boy was Skippy.

As more and more kids crowded around us, I realized I had two choices. I could stand my ground based on my innocence, laugh in Jeff's face, and run like the wind before I got chased, tackled and cajoled into doing the deed anyway; or I could scoff at his immature game, pretend I couldn't be intimidated, and announce that a playground dare didn't rattle me and neither did any four-eyed, pimple-pussed brainiac. I chose the latter. Besides, I reasoned, if I did what Jeff wanted, Jenny would know and I'd remain part of the Blue Coven, fulfilling my prime directive of belonging.

Then and there, I adopted the attitude that announced to my detractors, "Who here is braver or more daring than me? You'll all know how amazing I am after this."

Amid the roar of heckling and laughter, I mentally tried to quell my trembling hands and knees, but to no avail. I sank to the playground, face to face with Skippy, gazing at me in the moonlight, a look of goofy adoration on his face. "Good god," I thought. "There is *no* way!" But I knew, too, there was no way around it. I *had* to kiss Skippy. With an intimidating number of kids looming over me, escape was impossible.

In that moment, I feared my life was coming to an end. The last face I'd ever see would not be my mother's, but Skippy's.

In deep contemplation, I stared at Skippy. His gaping, wolf-like grin dripped spittle. Or maybe that was just my imagination, which was out of control with visions of his pimples exploding all over me. I couldn't help worrying that if the pus splashed on my skin, the contagion would cause a zit pandemic on my face. My mind burned with impossible exit strategies because my prayer, "Come on, God, really?" seemed to fall on deaf ears. I was sure it wasn't because I only spoke to Him when I was desperate. God's supposed to be around all the time, isn't He?

I finally surrendered, imagining Rhett Butler and Scarlet O'Hara in *Gone with the Wind*. I tilted my head back and waited for impact, as Skippy's face grew ever larger.

I had no idea how to kiss and feared his vile touch. The idea of his tongue touching mine made me cringe. My friend Jackie had warned me about a boy's tongue and the outpouring of saliva.

As our lips brushed together, every part of my physical body abandoned me, leaving me ill part in fear of my reputation and regret that my this kiss would be my last.

That's when Jeff, spurred by a burgeoning audience, added a new element to the game. My skin crawled as the first flings of wet playground mud smacked Skippy and me in our faces. With mud in my eyes, I squinted at brown globs of muck dripping from Skippy's thick glasses, down his nose, and into his crooked mouthful of teeth as he grinned stupidly. Was he actually *enjoying* this torture?

Why hadn't I taken the easy route and run home? Why were these people I called my friends making a mockery of me? To add insult to injury, now Skippy and I would be cemented together forever in junior high history: two classic nerds, kissing on center stage for the whole world to cackle at. The spectacle of our mud flogging would be tattooed on the lips of public academia in perpetuity, guaranteed to get worse with each exaggerated retelling.

In the murky darkness, I saw light in the idea of being kicked out of junior high so I'd never have to look these people in the eyes again. I'd be free, maybe even accelerated into high school because of my superior academic achievements. Skippy would probably be seen as the hero, taking one for the team, sacrificing his dignity for the sake of art, entertainment, and the girl he crushed on. Could I see myself being celebrated for this stunt? Would *my* peers look on me with awe and say, "Wow, I can't believe you did that!" Would I be idolized like Jenny?

The illusion disappeared with the next blow of mud to Skippy's ear. This one oozed down his cheek and plopped onto his shirt. And still he smiled. I could not. I was with my worst nightmare. We were in it together, yet Skippy was experiencing something completely different than I: despite the awkward circumstances, he was with the girl of his dreams.

In that moment and over the next two years of junior high, I never saw the real beauty of the adolescent boy I knew as Skippy. I couldn't muster the courage to see past the imperfections I saw in him— imperfections which mirrored my own. I couldn't give him the chance of love he longed for. But during high school, Skippy blossomed. He grew into his awkward pubescent features and transformed himself from the Four-eyed dork to Greek god with all the charisma a girl could dream of. I couldn't have known on that moonlit junior high playground that he would become one of the most popular, sought-after boys in high school. Otherwise I might have prevented the first of many regrets about my relationships with the opposite sex.

I know of women who are happily married to the man they met when they were kids. Or those that found their true love in college. That sort of thing never happened to me.

Over a decade later I ran into Skippy. The compelling Superman-esque jawbone still topped a body that would have made even Arnold sneer. He had changed his name and developed into a successful entrepreneur who traveled the world in his own private jet. Just as our awkward conversation was about to end, his gorgeous wife and angelic (red-headed) four-year-old daughter walked up. Words escaped me as I began to fantasize that I could have been in *this* life.

Guilt came upon me, as well as considerable regret. Had I really thought all those awful things about this gentle soul? Had I been so shallow as to not see the potential underneath this man's skin? What else in life had I missed by being superficial and absorbed with trying to fit in? I pulled my mind back into reality and said polite words, congratulating him on his success and family. As we parted I took one last glimpse of this epic creature, only to see that child-like grin, crooked teeth and all.

Sometimes we find ourselves living life from the lens of possibility, while at other times our framework is well informed by our surroundings. In my 13-year-old imagination the creature called Skippy was something to avoid at all costs. He had earned geek status with the people I truly believed were the ones to know—the cool crowd. Now it is not certain by any means that Skippy was Mr. Right for me, but what *is* absolutely true is that I wasn't willing to give him a chance. My beliefs were informed by the social standards to which I had chosen to adhere. Let's be honest, those standards were dictated by a bunch of young minds without a clue about what really matters in life. To this day I believe that during that unimaginable kiss, Skippy extended unconditional love to me. Despite our predicament, the look he gave me suggested that what truly mattered most in his world was me. Who knows what might have happened had I held that gaze and returned something like honest curiosity and connection instead?

Lessons Learned

Withholding our projections based on opinion, belief, or conditioning allows us to see others in their best light and makes for a more honest and authentic human connection.

The popular vote does not mean you are winning. Live your truth. Make up your own mind. Your relationship with yourself will outlast every other relationship, so be true to it.

Get curious about who you are and give others the gift of the same opportunity. You never know who is behind the glasses (real or not) you are both wearing. Seek the truth.

Be prepared for surprises, life is full of them.

Questions for Reflection

- How often do we meet people to whom we react or whom we dismiss for no particular reason at all? Or consider those times in which other people's opinions have shaped our own?

- How often have you, dear reader, found yourself regretting your own fast-formed opinion of someone, when later you learned that you were completely wrong about who that someone was?

- What if we gave people a chance by being curious about who they are?

- What if we released our first-held assumptions until we knew, through real experience, what or who was really in front of us?

About Feroshia Knight

Feroshia Knight, MA, PCC is well known for her infectious energy and irrepressible laughter (she was dismissed from class more than once for her endless giggles). She thrives on releasing the imaginative spirit in pursuit of love, light and happiness championing all that dare to play and live life out loud. Feroshia is the founder of the Baraka Institute and Coach Training World, two global playgrounds for the expansion of human potential.

In her rare and precious spare time, Feroshia is an avid explorer of the natural world both by land and sea – often found hiking, kayaking, biking or snowboarding whenever possible in the Pacific northwest or abroad. She is proudly owned by a theatrical nine-pound rescued Chi-Weenie, named MoChee who also loves to dance to Lady Gaga and sing (howl) along with his favorite tunes by her side.

www.barakainstitute.com | www.coachtrainingworld.com
www.feroshia.com

Transformation
as an Evolutionary Process
by Jennifer Blakley

My first memory of longing for connection and wanting transformation was around the age of seven. I went to Catholic school and was told fantastical stories of God communicating with ordinary people, telling them their purpose and giving them direction. He spoke directly through a burning bush and indirectly through angelic messengers, prophets and, ultimately, his Son. I remember thinking, "Of course these people had faith, their experience with God was direct! They saw miracles!" I was sitting in church wondering why God seemed to stop talking to us in recent years. Were we no longer worthy? Did he no longer care? The Catholic nuns assured me that God still spoke to us through messengers and gave me the example of when the Virgin Mary appeared to three children at Fatima in 1917. That seemed recent enough and I immediately began to wonder, "What was so special about those three children to whom Mary spoke? Why them?" I promptly concluded that I was clearly not good enough. "Maybe if I stare at the statues long enough and pray, they will talk to me? Maybe I could experience a miracle." Something in me yearned for a magical experience so profound that I believed, without a doubt, that all the stories were true and more importantly, that I was special and of value.

You may be less than shocked to learn, the statues never spoke to me. Bummer for seven-year-old me.

As I grew to learn more about Catholicism I realized that wanting to be special was a sin and that pride was frowned upon. It was much better to be humble. "This must be my big problem!" I thought. So an inner conflict began. I wanted to know God personally, which I was told required humility and faith. At the same time, I wanted to be special and experience something profound and magical.

Part of what I longed for was certainty and it wasn't clear if the stories I was being told were true. I also wanted clear direction and understanding of my purpose in life. I was asking God, "Give me a sign that you are real. Tell me who I am and what it is that I have to offer. Do it in a miraculous way so that I will believe it's you."

In eighth grade, it was time to pick a patron saint to be our confirmation name as we confirmed our baptism and belief in the Catholic faith. I picked Antonette, the feminine version of St. Anthony, the patron saint of lost souls.

By the age of eighteen I walked out of church crying in the middle of a sermon on belief in Jesus as the only way into the Kingdom of Heaven. This was a major event for me as my family was very religious. My Grandmother taught me prayers to say when I couldn't sleep. We said Grace at every meal. We planned family vacations around attending church. My mother was a Eucharistic minister, taught CCD (Religious class for public school students) and was the Librarian at my Catholic school. To walk out of church and proclaim "I am never going back." was a big deal! The reality was that I just couldn't fake belief in all the dogma anymore. How could God be so loving, good and righteous, yet still condemn those without a belief in Jesus to an afterlife of eternal damnation?

I thought about other religions with which I was familiar. My boyfriend, whom I adored, was Jewish, and his family was very loving. My late grandfather was Jewish as well. Did my mom believe her father was in hell? What about Gandhi? Was God sending his followers to hell? As an adoptee, I had the awareness that I could have been raised by a family of a different faith, and thus could have grown up with different religious practices and a different world view. My existential longing began as I questioned these and all religious teachings that claimed to have the only truth and way to salvation or enlightenment

In my twenties I completely cast religion aside. I just wanted to be happy and experience joy. A typical student in Santa Barbara, California, I was bright, capable and completely lost. I did have some wonderful friendships, yet something was always missing. I distracted myself from an underlying yearning for truth and deep loving connection through drinking, dancing, humor, and of course, boys. Intellectually, I enjoyed social sciences including sociology, psychology and philosophy, but the rest of my life was chaos. My exercise regime consisted of nightclub dancing and running my butt off working behind a bar; my nutritional program consisted of margaritas, Ding Dongs and Taco Bell; my meditation practice was lying on the beach with music blaring in my headphones. Eventually this lifestyle took a toll on my energy; by twenty-six, I rebounded out of a long-term relationship into a whirlwind romance. I got married, moved to Portland, Oregon and divorced within a year.

The end of my short marriage got me thinking. "What the hell is wrong with me?" Clearly, I longed for a deep connection and to experience unconditional love. At this point, I wasn't sure that unconditional love was possible. It was evident that my multiple-perspectives thinking style along with my habit of rolling from one experience to the next, made it hard to pick a side, trust one program, or make a permanent decision about anything.

Committing to one course of action was difficult, at best. Though my desire to understand all ways of being could be considered admirable by some, undirected, it was not useful for developing a strong identity and a clear sense of direction. It was time to make some changes.

I began to see a counselor, joined the Unitarian Universalist Church, volunteered my time with homeless youth and took up running and yoga. Though I was committed to working on myself, my social late-night tendencies were back in full force. The difference was that I traded in margaritas and Ding Dongs for fine wine and dark chocolate. This was far from a big shift, but I felt the beginnings of real personal growth. Eventually, I chose to earn a Master's Degree in Applied Theology in 2000, ironic considering my former renunciation of all things religious. Although I recoiled from anything that preached judgment and condemnation or claimed one true way to salvation, the Unitarian Church worked for me with its lack of dogma

and its commitment to social justice. Still, I felt compelled to begin
an interfaith pastoral counseling program at a Catholic university.
It looked at the effect of belief systems on mental and emotional
health—which was fascinating to me—and seemed a great way to
integrate my early experiences into a broader world view. My angst
with Catholicism was coming full circle and the healing began.

In 2002, while working on my degree--a process that took twice as
long as intended--I found my birth mother, married a big-hearted older
man with whom I had nothing in common, and became a stepmother
to two young ladies, ten and fourteen. Shortly after the wedding I gave
birth to my daughter. I was pregnant with my son when I eventually
finished my thesis and graduated in 2005.

I racked up quite a bit of life experience during the short period
I was in graduate school. I also began to notice a theme of paradox
during that time. In my life, painful and joyful experiences seemed to
walk hand in hand. My goal became to focus on lamenting the painful
that I missed experiencing the joyful. This was not always an easy task.

The birth of my first child was the most incredible, spiritually
intense, physically painful and emotionally joyful experience of my
life. I finally knew without a doubt that unconditional love truly
existed. As she grew, seeing the world through her eyes gave me
burgeoning spiritual insight. Unfortunately, a series of events that
began a few short months after her birth were causing severe distress
in my relationship with my husband. The joys of motherhood were
profound, but heartbreak, frustration, discontent, and resentment were
growing in my marriage.

No counselor, relationship book, or spiritual practice seemed
to help me meditate away the issues and feelings that were there.
Determined to make the marriage work, I vowed that if change were
possible I would find a way. Unfortunately, my status as a master of
distraction, and my strategy for putting negative feelings on the shelf
proved less than effective, especially when matched by my husband's
habits of avoidance and distraction. We had another child, a beautiful
boy, before the shelf full of negative feelings fell on my head with force.
I became very sick.

A desire to grow, heal myself and heal my family, led me to
approach my physical health with the same tenacity that propelled
my spiritual quest. Knowing the connection between body, mind

and spirit, I believed I had a huge block to uncover; my yearning to have optimal health in all areas of my life thus led me to participate in many workshops and to read many books. Some were insightful and inspiring, while others left me feeling a bit cynical. Visions of the *Saturday Night Live* character came to mind: "I'm good enough. I'm smart enough. And gosh darn it, people like me!" Had my life really come to this? Rolling my eyes and laughing at myself alternated with frustration and tears. The occasional cynicism aside, my nature remained optimistic and idealistic. Belief in the power of the human spirit to transcend the pitfalls of the human ego kept me open to life.

After sharing many of my insights and perspectives with friends, I was encouraged to become a life coach. I found this almost humorous and ironic considering my inner turmoil. I felt like a charlatan, yet I had a sense that spirit was leading me. I felt I had been in a dark night of the soul, in the process of deconstructing my ego, for years. Luckily, faith won out over insecurity. Putting my fear and self-judgement aside, I enrolled in Baraka Institute's Whole Person Coach training in 2007.

Training to become a life coach shook me to my core. Not only did I realize that my lifestyle did not fully represent my values, I also realized that I had many limiting beliefs holding me back from going for what I truly wanted. Some major changes ensued. The biggest and hardest decision was to leave the eight-year relationship that was literally making me sick. Our dysfunctional way of dealing with a mismatch of interests and values was not changing for the better. As I told my marital history to a counselor, it felt as if I were talking about somebody else's life. I concluded the narration of my drama saying, as if it had just occurred to me, "It's really bad isn't it?" Her response: "Lifetime movie bad!" Even with that kind feedback, it was hard for me to accept that with all I had learned, I still couldn't fix the situation. The relationship was teaching me how to set serious boundaries, how to exercise personal power, and the difference between giving up and letting go.

Terrified of hurting my children and being on my own as a single parent, I did not take the decision to divorce lightly. Ultimately, I realized that staying in an unhealthy situation, out of fear, was not the lifestyle I wanted to model for my children. Rather, I wanted them to learn to make decisions based in love. Underneath all the pain, I did love their dad. However, so much had happened during the course of our marriage that my trust was gone and my feelings were dead. Loving myself enough to leave a marriage that was draining my life energy became most important.

Committed to a peaceful outcome, the ensuing two-year divorce financially devastated and emotionally debilitated me in a way I had never before experienced. During the transformation, self-doubt hung around my neck like a noose; there was simply no way to deny negative feelings, no getting around the pain, no distraction from the inner terror. Everything was up for examination. Acceptance became the key to moving forward, allowing me to see things as they truly were.

My personal growth quickly intensified and my tendencies to compartmentalize pain and distract myself lessened a bit. While old habits die hard, at least I used healthier distractions at this stage in my life. I began studying compassionate communication, not just as a technique, but as a spiritual practice and got hooked on the results. This style of communication and conflict resolution helped me to focus on my feelings and the needs underlying the conflict. I became a more nurturing parent, sister and daughter. It also saved my divorce from becoming total combat.

Even today, compassionate communication helps me stay in a respectful friendship with my children's father. It has changed the way I experience views other than my own, giving me a healthy way to express negative feelings, rather than to repress them or react with anger. As I finally began learning the difference between conflict *resolution* and conflict *avoidance*, it became clear that I had gone through most of my life burying negative feelings, with no idea of my real needs. The awareness of how my thoughts and perceptions had contributed to my own discontent was growing.

Throughout my life I had only experienced mere glimpses of awareness and profound shifts in perception. Unfortunately, the experiences were usually short-lived. A feeling of permanent transformation and spiritual union seemed to elude me. I wondered: I have done so much work. Clearly I have grown! Were my habits of thinking *that* hard to break? Or was I subconsciously waiting for angels to descend and tell me that I had finally arrived? A silly as it sounds, part of me waited for something to happen that was so profound I could not deny its truth. I wanted to be one of those people who had visions, near-death experiences, spirits talking to them, or angels in their living room.

My search for truth and my strong need to contribute had led me to seek spiritual mentors, study the Enneagram, help homeless youth, speak on adoption panels, and volunteer on community service committees. While contributing to the well-being of others, I experienced more satisfaction, but I eventually got bored or disillusioned. Something always seemed to be missing. Eventually I realized that my underlying reasons for volunteering were centered on fixing myself or being a better "me." Contributing seemed a healthy thing to do, but I still searched for the thing that would give me an underlying sense of fulfillment, the mark of a life well-lived.

Even my hedonistic tendencies and desire for new interesting experiences were really about wanting to feel the intensity of being alive. Though an optimistic idealist on the surface, underneath I was dissatisfied with my ordinary day-to-day lifestyle. For me, only personal transformation held the promise of transcending a life of mediocrity. It took a while to realize that it was my thoughts and judgments about mediocrity that were causing my suffering.

Of all the many transformations I have undergone, the biggest was becoming a mother. It was exhausting, scary, and at times overwhelming; my life was no longer all about me. Life was joyful, loving and beautiful, a peak experience, yet so ordinary. This paradox brought me back to feeling genuine gratitude for all the wonderful gifts I had long taken for granted. Most importantly, I was ready to feel truly grateful for the gift of being alive.

When I look back on becoming a parent, I realize that as much as I loved becoming a mother, it was not an easy transition for a free spirit like me. The responsibility felt enormous. I had never been a worrier, at least not outwardly. Suddenly, I found myself anxious and worried on a regular basis. I was afraid of "screwing-up" as a parent. My fear and self-judgement co-mingled with an intellectual trust in the goodness of life and a maternal instinct that wanted nothing more than to nurture, protect and love.

As I reflect, step-parenting had challenged me more than I thought it would. I loved kids. I had been teaching seventh grade Sunday school at the UU church and working with homeless kids when I first met the girls who were then eight and twelve. I thought step-parenting would be a piece of cake. Unfortunately, my natural optimism did not fully prepare me for all the emotions involved. Marital stress and insecurity plagued me and although I loved my step-daughters, my role seemed superfluous. I struggled to connect with them and because of my ambivalence about my marriage to their father, I was uncertain if connecting was even the right thing to do. In the end I felt pretty insignificant in their lives. This perception caused me a lot of sadness.

I thought about the way I was raised. Like many of their generation, my parents were well-intentioned, ethical, hard-working, dutiful people who lacked empowering parenting skills and who seemed to rarely experience joy. They were not outwardly affectionate; while my mother showed moments of playfulness and enjoyed kids, my dad did not. Both regarded fear, punishment and guilt as valuable parenting tools, which was commonplace at the time, at least in my hometown.

A desire to learn from the past and raise happy, emotionally intelligent children consumed me as I read every parenting book on the shelf. Believing in the aphorism, "To learn, read. To understand, write. To master, teach," I eventually trained as a parent educator. I became a member of the International Network for Children and Families, mostly to master the techniques I had learned, but also to share what I found to be incredibly valuable information.

At a certain point, I realized that I was no longer a seeker but a finder. The finding came not from the education and tools I had received, though all were very useful. The finding came from going within myself, connecting to my higher consciousness and trusting inner intelligence to guide me. There was never one big shift that I could pinpoint as the day my life changed forever for the better. Rather, my life has been a series of awakenings leading to gradual changes that have opened me to a more compassionate experience of myself and others. The transformation I was seeking was really an evolution of consciousness. This evolution led me to discover the power and need of acceptance, non-judgment and the awareness of the oneness of humanity. This discovery has shifted both my experience of myself, and my experience of the world.

Acceptance has been one of the hardest things to grasp intellectually and emotionally. To me, it always felt more like giving up. It took a long time, for instance, to accept that my relationship with my children's father was never going to work. I now know that research has revealed that our brains don't function well when we are under stress. *And stress exists when our minds are resisting our reality.* This means that any time I am distracting myself from what I perceive as unpleasant, deciding whether something should or should not be happening, or trying to force change in others, I am resisting reality and am creating unnecessary stress for myself. At these times, nothing works.

Non-judgment is similar to acceptance. Judgment comes from the meaning we attach to whatever it is we are accepting or not accepting. Though I occasionally experience sadness over the loss of "what could have been had I known then what I know now," I don't have anger or resentment around it. It's all part of the learning. By humbly accepting my own shortcomings, I much more easily forgive others theirs. Over and over again I have realized that happiness, pro-activity, connection, love, positive change, and the good things that nurture life are all stifled by judgment of others and judgment of self.

Though I once prided myself on being fairly accepting and open-minded, my spiritual quest has helped me see all the stealth-like judgments I've let run my life. For example, judging judgmental people, instead of approaching them with curiosity and trying to understand why they hold a certain point of view, is one of the more difficult habits to recognize. Such attitudes cause emotional reactions, lower my energy and make me miserable.

As soon as I decide, "something is this way because..." or "this person has to change because..." or "this project will never work because..." I have eliminated understanding and squelched other possibilities. I have learned that if I come to a situation thinking, "Well, this is one way of doing things. What else might work more effectively?" I am not locked into a position and am not generating defensiveness, which can lock others into their position. When I come to a situation with an inner knowledge that there are many perceptions, I can generate more possibilities, more compassion and more acceptance. This way of approaching life creates far more inner peace and many more desirable outcomes. I realize that this sounds like a judgment in itself. Perhaps that is why the great masters speak in parables and ask questions.

I also discovered the truth, power and healing that can happen when we recognize how connected we are to others and the world as a whole. If we see ourselves as an extension of the collective, we come to understand that our basic human needs are never in conflict. To hurt or neglect someone else is to hurt or neglect oneself. It is in our own best interest, as a collective whole, to meet everyone's basic needs. It is only our perception of our separateness and our strategies to meet, at all costs, our own individual needs, that cause conflict.

We currently live in a "power over" world. The need for security and well-being, coupled with the fear of being overpowered by another human being, group or country can lead people to do hideous things to each other. Sadly, when two people are in battle, both often feel justified in going to any length see that their needs and the needs of "their people" are met. "Their people" are the ones who share the same beliefs, values and strategies for navigating life. Both sides think the other side is evil or inhuman, or at best tragically misguided, resulting in wasted or hoarded resources, and rules and regulations designed to "protect."

"Us vs. them" thinking comes from fear-based stories and beliefs we are raised with or that we create about life. We end up in conflict with our perceived enemies' stories and beliefs about life. And so the war begins. In contrast, the evolution of consciousness understands that we are all connected, that by valuing other people's needs as much as our own, we nurture all our lives.

I realize that under current global conditions, feeling our connection to everyone sometimes seems an impossible task. I try, therefore, to imagine a peaceful world where all of life is valued; a world where the "power over" shifts to a "power with" paradigm as we recognize our connectedness and honor many wonderful and varied expressions and lifestyles. The alternative to collectively evolving is to ultimately destroy the planet as we fight with one another, bomb each other, and squander our precious resources on the few, while millions starve.

How do I, a mere drop in the ocean, take on this seemingly impossible task of evolution?

I believe world peace begins with healing ourselves, a view embodied perfectly in the famous quote by Mahatma Gandhi, *"We must be the change we wish to see in the world."* Individual change leads people in many different directions. I feel a strong desire to support other parents with skills that empower children and create an environment of mutual respect and cooperation. If world peace begins with healing ourselves, then it must begin in the home. Our children are the next generation of leaders, whether they are actually leading society, or subtly affecting the world by the way in which they live. Therefore, we have a huge responsibility to raise them in a manner that positively affects the future of the world.

When we parent our children by using "power over" techniques--"my way or the highway" and "do it because I said so"--we put them at risk either to become compliant, always bending to the will of others; or to manipulate others to get what they want. One way or the other they will be looking outside themselves for approval, trust and fulfillment.

When we are apathetic about their emotions or blind to their experience, we teach our children to scream louder or shut down. As a rather compliant person who shut down emotionally very easily, I know first hand that this way of being only breeds resentment and frustration.

I have also witnessed the "power over" syndrome; I have observed and coached individuals who are considered very successful by societal standards, but whose personal relationships are tragic. What I have seen is that those who are the most successful *and* fulfilled operate from the "power with" perspective. They see the unique attributes offered by each individual, while understanding our essential connectivity and oneness. They empower everyone around them. Indeed, the most influential beings in history have been powerful while modeling compassion and empathy, allowing similarities and connectedness to reveal themselves.

I now feel called to synthesize all that I have learned from my master's program, life coaching certification, parent educator certification, and compassionate communication mediation training, life experience, as well as the many spiritual development seminars I have attended. My goal is to help individuals and families learn to transform conflict--within themselves, with one another, and with the world around them--into true connection, compassion and love. I want to help people to truly nurture themselves. For when we nurture ourselves and share ourselves with the others, we are healing the world.

Now that I am a finder, I realize that I have been seeking what many others seek: a happy life, a life well-lived, vibrant health, intimacy, a sense of belonging, joy and adventure. So many long for these things, yet these basic goals still elude the vast majority. The self-help industry is booming, right alongside record pharmaceutical drug sales. Perhaps the problem is the mistaken belief that we are separate; that personal growth is just that: personal. If more people truly believed their personal transformation was necessary to heal the world, wouldn't they be more diligent in this spiritual pursuit? What if people also realized that the swiftest path to personal fulfillment was to freely and joyfully help others? How different our world would be.

We continue evolving as a collective. This evolution of collective consciousness is about feeling both the connection to ourselves and to all of life. When I am living from connection, I choose to nurture others in the best way that I know how. Genuinely feeling my connectivity to the people around me has led to an understanding that my growth is not just about me. I am more aware than ever that when I raise my energetic vibration to express more love and joy, I uplift others in the process. The more awareness, love and joy that I embody, the more positive effect I have on others, who "pay it forward" as well. Lovingly offering service, free of self-sacrifice, to the greater whole, brings me fulfillment and inner peace. When I shift my focus from "What do I want in my life?" to "What energy do I want to offer the world?" happiness is the by-product.

I am no longer waiting for a miracle to prove the existence of God or to validate my status as a chosen one. We are all chosen! We are chosen to recognize our gifts and our interconnectedness. Whether that unique gift is love, joy, peace, wisdom, creativity or empowerment, each of us is chosen to authentically radiate who we are. We are called to have compassion and to bring healing energy to those who struggle to see their own light.

Do I still want statues to talk to me? Of course!

Questions for Reflection

- How would you relationships change if you completely embraced non-judgment and acceptance?

- Is this possible? What would be challenging?

- What would it feel like to be more accepted by others? Yourself?

About Jennifer Blakley

Jennifer Blakley MA CPC is a Family and Communication Skills Coach. She has combined her education and training in Pastoral Counseling, Relationship Mediation, Parenting and Life Coaching to create transformational process called Peaceful Solutions.

She has a strong desire to support parents struggling with various family issues like divorce, step-parenting and adoption. Peaceful Solutions is designed to help individuals and families make peace with the past, learn skills for the present and create a future of fulfillment. Jennifer believes that the way we parent our children will have a tremendous influence on creating a more peaceful world.

www.JenBlakleyCoaching.com

You CAN Teach an Old Dog
New Tricks

by Jeanette Emmons

How different would my life have been over the past fifty years if I had actually made choices from my authentic self instead of my conditioned self? Of course, a child of ten--and yes, I'm sixty now--hardly knows the difference between the two. I didn't know until several years ago when I became acquainted with the terms "core values" and "belief systems."

When I narrow this "authentic self vs. conditioned self" question down even further, I find new questions: What would my life have been like if, at a very early age, I knew that I created my own reality? What if, as a child, I knew that my mind was unique and that whatever I filled it with was unique to me, myself alone. I could then have set goals and reached them. In this perfect world, my parents would have sat me down for a conversation that would have gone something like this:

"Honey, our family is unique. We have a special program that is developing in our brains. What you will be experiencing as you live in this household, is *our* particular family belief system. As you grow up, this will influence you and your relationship to the world outside our family.

"Now, other families have different belief systems. When you talk with others, you might hear them express other ways of thinking. This is good! There is no right or wrong, just another interpretation of the world around you. Be curious. Ask questions. Learn from others as they encourage you to expand your mind.

"You will also have feelings when you talk to other people and experience your presence with them. Sometimes you will feel good, and other times what they say will make you feel not so good. These feelings you have are called emotions and they can help guide you through life. The challenge is to interpret them accurately."

Well, my parents never had this conversation with me and I never had this conversation with my own children. However, I have had this dialogue with my grandchildren and now I have it daily with myself. You see, you *can* teach an old dog new tricks, and that old dog is me!

So my story begins…

For several years I courted the idea of becoming a life coach. I was unhappy with my job and yet I believed strongly that I was responsible for creating my own reality. Because of movies such as "The Secret" and books like "Leveraging the Universe" and "Engaging the Magic" by Mike Dooley, I knew I had to do something to start the shift forward with a more positive plan for my future. I enrolled in Baraka's Whole Person Coach training in March of 2009.

Several months into the program, I realized that the information and practice was becoming more about my own personal growth. I struggled emotionally through the six month long training, but I was determined to change my belief system regarding negative self worth and my ability to share my gifts with the world.

One of the biggest "aha" moments of my life occurred during coach training in a weekend session of the third month. All my doubts and fears about myself culminated in an anxiety attack. While a few emotional challenges were going on in my life, I had never experienced these sensations in my body before. My heart felt so heavy that I could barely breathe and the thoughts in my mind were unsettling. I felt that everyone in the class was aware of the intensity of the emotions I was feeling.

At the break I confessed my situation to my teachers. That is an interesting word, confess. And my weakness in that moment was an embarrassment to me. I even discussed the idea of quitting the program and resuming at a later time. They held such a comforting and compassionate space for me as I cried. I felt safe. I learned then what an important part active listening plays in life coaching. It was certainly important for me, at that time, to be heard.

My peer coaches and teachers told me that they would support any decision I made. Additionally, they posed some powerful questions around the outcome of my resolution: What will you **gain** by leaving? What will you **lose** by leaving? What **effect** will your decision have upon you?" they inquired.

With these questions presented to me, I suddenly realized my habit of quitting when I felt strong negative emotions. Self-sabotage had kept me "safe". But it had also prevented me from becoming all that I could be. As Caroline Myss affirms in her book, "Sacred Contracts," "The Saboteur archetype is made up of the fears and issues related to low self-esteem that causes you to make choices in life that block your own empowerment and success"

I first remember my own saboteur at work while I was a child in the early sixties. The scene is a grade school softball field in early spring of 1961. I'm eleven years old and I'm standing in right field during softball tryouts. My eyes are glued to the batter's box waiting for the player to make contact with the next pitch.

"Oh, here it comes! The ball is heading my way!" I have my glove positioned high over my head to catch it. "Oops! I missed it!"

From out of nowhere comes a chorus of voices beginning to chant, "Emmons missed the ball! Emmons missed the ball!" I turn around to identify the voices and see Mike, Tim and Dana, three boys from my class. They had been out of sight watching and waiting to tease us girls.

I doubt they had the intention to hurt me, but my self-esteem took a beating that day.

Pubescent boy and girl banter -- something so innocent-- created a very shameful incident for me. I was so upset that I didn't continue with the tryouts the next day. As I ponder this childhood memory, I wonder how many times before this incident did I get my feelings hurt and then back off to protect myself emotionally?

Another incident in my past comes to mind. It's 1960 and I am ten years old. The setting is a fifth grade classroom and the subject is English. The teacher is discussing our homework assignment, which is an essay on the theme "Spring." What's really exciting to me is that we are allowed to decorate our paper. Back in those days, children's creativity was allowed only during art class, so this assignment was special to me.

As I write this memoir, I think about the quality of effort that I always put into my homework. Even though I was just ten, I was conscientious of all that that I handed in. My papers were neat and handed in on time and this assignment was to be an example of the perfection that I demanded of myself.

I decided that my composition would center on the spring flowers blossoming for all to see and enjoy. One flower I was particularly fond of was the blue Iris, and my grandmother had a garden full of them. Their sturdy stems allowed them to stand regally and move with the wind, and I recounted this memory with my words: Yes, those beautiful "flags" that swayed back and forth. I was proud of my paper and anxious for my teacher to read my masterpiece.

My excitement quickly changed the following day. The teacher ignored the beautiful words I had crafted together, sharing my spring experience. Her attention to my work focused only on a mistake I had made in paragraph development. As she read my work in front of the class, the pride I felt for my story turned to shame. I all but disappeared from my seat in the classroom, emotionally traumatized.

You see, when the teacher read my composition, she didn't understand that the flags I referred to were flowers. She thought I was writing about the American Flag, which certainly did *not* belong in a paragraph about flowers! Instead of pointing out the positive, she used my story as an example of how not to write. Fortunately she did not tell the class that the paper belonged to me. But *I* knew and I was deeply shamed.

Humiliation, embarrassment, degradation, whatever label you want to give the emotion, it rattled my innocent little soul. Pretty powerful words, aren't they? It's no wonder that writer's block and more pain followed this childhood experience for so long.

Bringing these past experiences forward has helped me understand that childhood wounds have blocked personal growth in many areas of my life. Since training to be a life coach, I have learned to recognize my fears, where they come from, and how to move forward in spite of them. Now, in order to reach my goals, I use my fears as challenges. I understand that personal expansion is not available to me if I stay in the safety zone, I might feel comfortable, but there is no personal expansion here.

Choosing to write a chapter for this book was not an easy decision. I was uncomfortable putting my thoughts down on paper for anyone to read. The fear of getting less than a perfect "grade" was always in the back of my mind. Years of red marks and checks on the top of my notebook papers played on my subconscious like an out-of-tune sonata.

As I prepared to sit and write this chapter, I found many ways to procrastinate and sabotage my planned outcome, the goal of publishing my story. At times, I needed something to eat or drink. Other times, I would decide that my house was dirty and set about cleaning it. And those pesky whiskers on my chin seemed to constantly reappear for tweezing.

The biggest obstacle, however, was the little voice that told me I had no talent for writing. In the way each time I began to write, the comments would nag me about my prose being of little interest to anyone.

Now the old me, before training, would have believed that voice, but not the new me. Coaching experience helped me find a new voice in my head. In a much louder voice, I am reminded that I can do anything I focus on and put my energy toward.

The old belief system told me that I would open myself to painful criticism if I put pencil to paper. My new belief system, on the other hand, assures me that not everyone will like what I write, but my self-worth will remain unaffected by their assessment.

As I draw this story to a conclusion, I want you to know that there is a happy ending for several reasons. Were you doubtful? Self-introspection and personal growth is hard work, but with the proper tools, I have been able to maneuver my life journey with more awareness, intention and self-motivated direction. Each day gives me new choices to make that will lead me in the direction of my best life. As I stepped up to the challenge to write a chapter for this project, in the process I jumped over the low self-esteem hurdle and landed safely on my feet. I truly enjoyed the task and found it much easier than I thought possible, even working with Microsoft Word! Perhaps, I'll write something else, so keep your eyes on the New York Times Bestseller List. You may just see my name there in the future.

Postscript

In preparation for this writing, I looked up the Iris in Wikipedia. This is what I found:

"*Iris versicolor*, also commonly known as the Harlequin Blueflag, Larger Blue Flag, Northern Blue Flag, and other variations of those names, is a species of Iris native to North America where it is common in sedge meadows, marshes and along stream banks and shores... The Blueflag is the provincial flower of Quebec, having replaced the Madonna Lily which is not native to the province."

In my composition all those many years ago I wasn't incorrect in my usage of the moniker "flag" for my flower. The teacher just didn't know her flowers as I did! You can imagine the emotional healing this information has provided.

Thank you, Authentic Self. You are so much more fun to have around than that old Conditioned Self!

Questions for Reflection

- Which part of your life do you feel needs changing?

- What childhood memory continually comes to mind that was an emotionally charged experience for you?

- How might this experience be related to the part of your life seeking change?

About Jeanette Emmons

Jeanette Emmons, CPC lives in Milwaukie, Oregon with her father, and her Boston Terrier, Ruby.

Since retiring from the corporate world in 2010, Jeanette keeps herself busy as a volunteer for Providence Hospice and the Milwaukie Senior Center. Besides her family, the Baraka community also continues to be a focal point in her life.

Jeanette sees herself as a "late bloomer" who continually welcomes new and challenging life experiences. She believes the best is yet to come.

www.alchemylifecoaching.com

Drusilla
& the Sharks

by Kristen Karle

Sharks? What sharks? I didn't even *think* about the possibility of sharks on my dream vacation to the Sea of Cortez.

"Oh don't worry," my kayaking guide said. "They'll probably leave you alone."

I'm terrified of sharks. But I was also hot, I mean really hot. The sun was blazing onto the pristine white beach with absolutely no shade. That was another thing that hadn't occurred to me in my months of fantasizing about this trip.

As I stood shin deep in the crystal clear turquoise water, a familiar voice from within said, "How the hell did you get into this? You're camping for a week with ten people you don't know, in the blazing hot sun of Baja, Mexico, and the water has sharks in it! What were you thinking?!"

Oh, that voice. That voice has been with me my entire life. The one that is so fearful, so stuck, so hard on me, so worried about being perfect, so ever-present, so *loud*!

This voice, my inner critic, has earned an actual name: Drusilla. She wears a scratchy wool military uniform and is equipped with whistle and whip just in case things ever get out of line. She never takes a fifteen-minute break, let alone a vacation, and she wasn't about to let me relax on this one.

So how exactly did I get here on the edge of this blazing hot beach with shark-infested waters complete with my inner Drusilla shouting in my head?

It started months before in a non-descript white room. I sat in front of a small group of life coaches-in-training, happily volunteering to be someone's model client. I believe the emphasis was on helping someone to create a plan. "How about planning a vacation?" Jane, my peer coach, suggested.

"Sure. Sounds great!" I responded. Sitting in the client chair, I felt totally relaxed, ready to get going.

"So Kristen, I understand you'd like to take a vacation. Have you decided where you'd like to go?"

"I can't take a vacation!" The words tumbled out of my mouth before I could even think. This exercise was supposed to be about planning, not resistance. But I couldn't help it. Drusilla was front and center and *very* determined. Her words became mine in the session.

"There is no way I can go on vacation. I don't have the money; I'm too busy to take the time off work; my boss won't let me; I don't want go anywhere alone; and I don't have anyone to go with."

In short, I was absolutely convinced there was *no* possible way I could take a vacation. I ended up in tears. Yeesh...

I apologized to Jane while our instructor cleverly used the experience as an example of how something seemingly "simple" could trigger a whole bunch of resistance and other topics to explore.

Driving back from the training left me two hours alone in the car. Perfect. Two hours alone with Drusilla, and I also made some time to beat myself up for letting Drusilla run wild. Hadn't I done enough personal work to get rid of her? What about all those therapy sessions, the energy work, and journaling? Not to mention all those personal growth books I had devoured? Why was she still around? Why wasn't I fixed yet?

At some point, I lost track of beating myself up and got caught up listening to music instead. I finally began to relax. Out of nowhere, something popped in my brain. "I want to be somewhere sunny and warm doing yoga and sea kayaking. *That's* what I want." I felt calm and clear, totally at peace and convinced-- for about a millisecond--it would happen.

That's when Drusilla chimed in, "How the heck would you do that? You don't have equipment, you don't really even know how to kayak, and it would be too expensive. What a bizarre combination! Yoga and kayaking? That is something you could do if you had a boyfriend, but you're single, so no way. You have too many things going on at work. Your boss would *never* be okay with you leaving now."

The next morning, I arrived at work and gradually settled into a Monday. Out of curiosity, I Googled "Yoga and Sea Kayaking." The first search result was a company based out of British Colombia specializing in wellness travel and retreats.

Hmmm, interesting. I honestly didn't know such travel companies existed. When I was growing up, the only travel we did was an annual hop in the 1978 Chevy Malibu to make the nineteen-hour drive to visit my great-grandparents in Florida. The idea of a travel company that takes care of all the details of vacationing in an exotic place was a totally foreign concept to me.

What's more, the travel company had an upcoming trip that was a yoga and sea kayaking adventure to Baja, Mexico, led by two women. They would teach yoga class, cook all the meals, and guide us in the kayaks. Everything was provided and all I had to do was show up. The cost was very reasonable. Although I was still convinced I didn't have money for such an extravagance, I decided to e-mail the contact person to get more details. I wanted to know: was this trip for beginners and did I really just need to show up? Yes and yes. And the woman at the travel company was wonderful. I had a warm, fuzzy, relaxed feeling just from e-mailing with her.

Even though Drusilla was reminding me that my quest was absurd and utterly impossible, I decided to look at plane tickets for the dates. The flight from my hometown to the Baja destination was available for a very reasonable price. Interesting, and yet I still wasn't convinced the trip was feasible.

I traipsed over to my co-worker's office to share, in a defeated tone, "I found this yoga/sea kayaking trip to Baja, but I don't have the money to do it."

Her response: "Kristen you *have* to do it! Have you done your taxes yet?"

"Not yet. Forgot about those…"

Well, everything aligned from there. I did my taxes that night and realized that my refund would more than cover the trip.

I made a plan of attack to get my work done. Another co-worker was so thrilled about my potential adventure that she offered to cover for me at an important meeting.

My boss didn't even blink when I asked him for the time off. He was actually happy for me. Things were falling into place perfectly. Obviously this was meant to be and now it would be smooth sailing from here on out.

Or would it?

For the next ten weeks the voices in my mind took turns reminding me that my trip was going to be either "the best thing ever" or "the worst idea I'd ever had!"

Ten full weeks of back and forth. All my friends were so excited for me. It seemed like no one could relate to my anxiety.

"Who gets anxious about vacations? You're such a freak!", Drusilla offered.

The day of the trip, I was a total wreck. My uber-adventurous, ultra-outdoorsy roommate drove me to the airport. Somehow that seemed to exacerbate my anxiousness.

"Aren't you *totally* excited? Getting out of Eugene in March to go somewhere sunny! I'm so jealous," he said.

"Yeah, totally excited!" I lied through my teeth.

"Have a great time! I know you will!" he said as we pulled into the drop-off area.

"Uh-huh…yeah. Thanks for the ride." I was almost in tears. I felt more like I was a child being shipped off to summer camp for the first time rather than an adult choosing a vacation. Maybe that was part of my problem. I'd never been to summer camp. Maybe that would've helped.

Two days later and there I was: toes digging into white sand, feeling more fear and dread than I ever imagined possible on a beach resembling paradise. And then something totally unexpected happened.

Another voice—calmly, gently—came forward from within. "You're here. It is absolutely beautiful. You have a choice about how you experience this. You can stay in fear or you can let go and just experience it for what it is. You're here, on an island that you reached by kayak. You can't really leave. It's your choice—fear or let go."

At that moment I took several steps deeper into the water, closed my eyes, held my breath and dove in—into the clear, refreshing, majestic Sea of Cortez—sharks and all. I swam the strokes I'd been swimming since I was a kid and experienced the unique feeling of submission that only happens when you're immersed in water. It seemed like I swam underwater for some time, but in reality it was probably only a few seconds, as Drusilla was lurking in the back—okay, middle—of my mind, reminding me of the sharks.

When my head came out of the water, I heard the screams from the shore. "Oh my God! Look!" My moment of bliss subsided as I immediately assumed I was being approached by a shark, about to die a tragic death, or at least suffer horrible wounds after a long, hard-fought struggle. But when I stood up in the water, (told you I didn't swim that far) I saw not sharks, but dolphins! Real, actual dolphins. Several of them.

They were swimming by as dolphins do; nose, fin and back coming out of the water, swirling up and out of the water, one after the other, like a dolphin dance. So graceful, so beautiful and so right in front of *me!* With the exception of visits to Sea World, this was as close as I'd ever been to dolphins. Fifty feet from me. In the same water as me. Me? Things like this didn't happen to me! Things like this happen to Other People.

A few moments before, I was in paradise, crabby and scared, unable to appreciate the opportunity all around me. Yet despite my fear, I dove in the water and the universe gave me the gift of seeing a pod of dolphins!

I stood in the water and watched those dolphins until I could no longer see them. I swam around, venturing further from the shore, gaining trust in myself, in the universe and in letting go and giving in to the experience.

I wish I could say from that moment on I was instantly transformed; that Drusilla fell silent; that there was no more fear; that I adored everyone in the group and every part of the trip. But that wouldn't be true. Throughout the journey, Drusilla made her presence known.

While I stood in Mountain Pose on a rocky cliff over the sea, trying to ground my energy into the earth, Drusilla whined relentlessly, "This isn't enjoyable, this is painful. The rocks are poking through the yoga mat and digging into your feet!"

Sitting in quiet meditation, smelling the salty morning air, Drusilla had her own chant that went something like, "Why are you sitting here doing absolutely nothing? You're a privileged, over-educated snob."

Yet as the days went on, the trip offered experiences aimed at showing me—and Drusilla—that incredible things can happen to us.

One day, we were getting ready to leave our camp to kayak to our next destination. One of our guides asked the group if we wanted to try to use the power of intention to summon a blue whale since we would be crossing their migration path. A sighting seemed unlikely since she hadn't seen one all spring. The group was slightly shy about it; Drusilla was not optimistic at all.

Nevertheless, being in yoga mode we all got into a circle and started chanting, "Blue whale, blue whale, blue whale." Our spiritual circle eventually took on the vibe of a football huddle. We were all laughing hysterically by the time we broke and ran to our boats, buzzing with excitement about the possibility of our upcoming encounter with the largest mammal on earth.

Halfway through the crossing, as the excitement had begun to wane, our guide exclaimed, "Look!"

And there it was, the massive shape coming out of the water directly ahead of us. I don't know exactly how close we were, but if it had wanted to change directions and come toward us, it would have been there in seconds. I was transfixed by this amazing creature, how it moved through the water so fast, how it was just so immense, and how we were in the very same sea.

The universe was really trying to make its point. And it did. As I spent more time meditating, relaxing, napping, doing yoga, paddling, and chatting with my tripmates, Drusilla spoke less and less often. And when she did, the other gentler voice also whispered, just loudly enough that I could actually hear her.

Of course it makes sense that in paradise, with no outside stress, Drusilla would calm down. Seeing the sun rise and set everyday, listening to the water, being away from all the distractions of the modern world, helped to quiet Drusilla.

But the trip did eventually have to end.

On the plane ride home from Los Angeles to Eugene, I sat in my seat, still reveling in the bliss, noticing the relaxed state of my normally super-tense body. I replayed fresh memories from the trip and jotted them down, along with my revelations, hoping not to forget them.

And then, Drusilla reappeared. "See, I don't know why you got yourself so worked up. Everything was great!" Instead of getting upset that she had returned, I found myself smiling and responding to her with kindness (in my head, of course).

"Oh there you are! Thanks for your input. Maybe you can relax a bit and enjoy the flight. We'll do the crossword in the airline magazine in a second. Your critical eye is very good at those."

It would be nice if I could say that my life was completely transformed from that point on. It wasn't.

But my life did change.

The change was that I began to understand and accept my process. I have learned that for me, transformation isn't a one-shot, instant shift. I used to get frustrated that change didn't happen swiftly enough, but now I can see that it's an ongoing practice. I have to consciously choose to nurture and take care of myself; to acknowledge Drusilla when she shows up instead of resisting her, which only makes her more critical; to really listen for my authentic voice, and to trust it, even when what it tells me seems scary. I've also learned that I can actually ask my authentic voice for her opinion, rather than just waiting around hoping to hear from her.

The trip also taught me that when I take care of myself, and I mean really, truly nurture myself, fear subsides and I am able to hear my true voice more clearly. Self-care doesn't have to mean taking a week off work and heading to a secluded paradise. It doesn't even mean sitting in lotus position for hours on end.

My self-care practice includes: getting enough sleep, exercising, spending time with people I love, reading great books, laughing as often as possible, learning new things, breathing deeply, using nice-smelling lotion, cheering on my favorite hockey team, cooking delicious meals, listening to great music, going for walks, watching the sunset and the list goes on.

I actually do have a list. I made it so that when I am stressed and can't figure out what's next, I can reach for the list instead of ice cream. And the list has led me to an actual practice. I have found that I need to do some things on a regular basis, while others just seem right at a given moment. The whole purpose is to do something, anything, no matter how small, with the intent of nurturing myself every day.

My old patterns still show up, reminding me that I must learn my core lessons over and over again, each time getting to a deeper level. That is *my* process. Now, instead of getting frustrated, I check in to see which things might be off and where I'm not taking care of myself enough. All the years of personal work and everything that I've learned, have enabled me to build a foundation to which I come back to often.

On my refrigerator I have a photo that captures the dolphin day beach. Most of the time I just glance at it, but sometimes I actually see it and am reminded that when I take a risk and dive in, even if I'm terrified, I'm sometimes rewarded with dolphins. And if I'm really lucky, maybe even blue whales.

Questions for Reflection

- What voices make a running commentary on your life?

- Who are they? What do they look like? Sound like? How could you change your relationship with them?

- What are some risks you've taken? How did it turn out? How did you feel?

- How do you truly nurture yourself?

About Kristen Karle

Kristen Karle is passionate about the art and science of "change-making". With over a decade of experience in the field of sustainable community development she assists individuals and leaders to build healthy, positive, sustainable changes in their life through self-awareness, self-esteem and self-care.

Her commitment to self-mastery brought her to the Baraka Institute in 2007 in pursuit of her Whole Person Coach Certification.

Kristen's unique blend of life experience and professional expertise enables her to support a myriad of clients to find clarity and develop tangible life plans. Never one to shy away from depth and true meaning, she works collaboratively with clients to explore deeply held beliefs, values, and patterns that previously prevented them from being their best self.

She is delighted to work with others in identifying and fully living their passions with an eye on creating 'self care practices' that enable them to explore and nurture these passions. She loves seeing her clients experience how doing the 'little things' for themselves can have profound impacts in their lives.

www.ousialiving.com

An Uneventful Near-Death

Experience

by Michelle Barry Franco

The blue streak sliced across my windshield like a silent scream.

Dazed and disoriented, I shifted my focus to the rearview mirror, frantic for a view of the top of my three-month-old infant's peach-fuzzed head. The air in the car turned hot and thick, my lungs too narrow to breathe it in deeply. My peripheral vision hazed over as if to protect me from the traumatizing view out either side. The world turned into a slow-motion movie as I pulled my rearview gaze to the right and then slowly left, petrified at the horror I was certain I'd see.

Except there was nothing.

The cars on either side of me were moving along as though nothing had happened. The paintbrush cloud streaks in the bright blue sky were unaffected, un-riled, still. The radio voice from the stereo hung in the thickness of the car's interior.

The man in the car to my right mouthed the words to a song on the radio, tapping his fingertips on the steering wheel in time with the music. On the other side of me, a woman eased her car into the left turn lane. On autopilot, I pushed my foot steadily on the brake to line up behind the cars ahead of me at the red stoplight.

I whispered to the sound of my baby's unaffected breathing, "We almost just died."

I have no idea how many near-death experiences I've had in my life. Do you? How can we? But on a Saturday afternoon, nearly five years ago, I had one. I watched a violently speeding vehicle narrowly miss folding my car door into my intestines. The difference between life and death was a mere fraction of a second. If I hadn't insisted on those last hugs from my older daughters in my husband's car in the pizza parlor parking lot that day, my infant daughter and I would not be here now.

Maybe the difference between this kind of near-death experience and the kind where your car actually rolls off the side of an icy road, is that your mind can pretend that it wouldn't have been that bad. Sometimes my mind does this, tries to tell me the story that the blue car wasn't actually driving that fast, or wasn't as close to slicing our car in two as I see it in my memory. My clever brain even goes so far as to question whether the experience actually happened. But that doesn't work because my heart, my soul and my gut all *know* that everything nearly ended that sunny Saturday afternoon.

Long before my life flashed across my windshield that day, my sister asked me if I'd ever had some kind of near-death experience when I was young. She wondered where I got my urgency to live each day to its greatest potential. It is true that I have always been inclined to ask, "Are we really sure we *can't* do that?" I tend to push the edges of possibility, to look for ways to experience life outside the status quo.

Possibly it's a genetic thing, or maybe it's a direct result of childhood experiences. When you grow up in a family mired in alcohol and drug addiction and yet survive childhood, it's a safe bet that you've had a fair share of near-misses through accidents and neglect.

As a kid, I once leapt out of a vehicle driven by a completely obliterated drunk adult—one who was supposed to be caring for my siblings and me—into the middle of a busy four lane road. Not long before that horrible day, I remember squeezing my eyes tight to the oncoming traffic lights as a *different* drunk adult in my life drove my thirteen-year-old cousin and me the wrong way onto a freeway off-ramp.

I suppose I had been primed my whole life to notice such experiences, to be poignantly aware of the fragility of my life.

Yet the truth of the matter is, I had never actually pushed the edges that far. Yes, I had traveled more than others in my family. I had quit solid jobs that I didn't like very much—good jobs that paid the bills and had great ladder-climbing potential—to find my passion in work. I'd moved out of state with my partner, neither of us knowing a soul in our new town nor having any idea how we would pay our bills long-term.

So maybe I had made some decisions that people in my life felt were risky and unusual. But really, I'd never done anything that felt viscerally scary to me. So far, my decisions had all been relatively safe ways of convincing myself I was living a courageous life.

That's because I had never knowingly, *absolutely* experienced the moment between life and death, until that Saturday afternoon.

I wish I could say that everything became clear immediately following that silently screaming blue car, that my life's purpose fell fully-formed into my consciousness. I wish I could say that my whole life changed dramatically in that moment. That would make for a nice big turning point in my story.

But it didn't. Instead, I drove the seven minutes it took to get home. I remember carrying our baby in the worn grey sling, walking from the driveway to tread the four wood steps up to our kitchen door. I remember seeing my husband through the half-window in that door, the sun shining in beautiful, warm yellow streaks across him and onto the floor where my three-year old daughter stood telling him something, or more likely, making a request. He was leaning down and forward a bit, gently smiling, our eighteen-month-old playing with the flip-flops strewn about near our ever-unkempt shoe bins. There were dishes piled next to the sink and on the cutting board a kiwi fruit sat waiting to be sliced.

"If I had not insisted on that last hug in that parking lot, he would be getting a phone call right now," I thought to myself. My heart squeezed into the size of a raisin.

The very thought of it all was more than my psyche could handle. I walked into the kitchen where my husband stood with our two older daughters and I gave them each a breezy "hello" kiss. I tucked the story into a small pocket behind my slowly rehydrating heart.

It was weeks before I felt enough distance from that uneventful life-altering moment to share it with anyone. It's the kind of story that feels like a new trauma every time I say it out loud. It's just as well, because on the rare occasions in which I have shared the story, I have felt the oceanic distance between the gut-level life alteration I experienced that day and my listener's ability to comprehend the impact it had on my life.

Who can blame them? *Nothing happened.*

I was not rushed to the hospital, the sound of sirens blaring in the background. I did not watch my life flash before my eyes as my car rolled across four lanes of highway. There was no bloody accident scene.

Playing Big

Yet, here's what happened inside me.

The place in my being that knows I can play bigger stepped forward. The part of me that always knew I had a meaningful contribution to make began to speak louder than the other part of me that was petrified to fail. The unconscious sense I have always had, that my life is not a "given," that any day can be my last, turned into a powerful *consciousness.*

It didn't happen right away. It happened slowly, with determination. It is still happening right now. Today.

In practical terms, I made some big life changes. Realizing that getting another degree was my easy way out, my safe bet, I quit a graduate school program that wasn't right for me. I already knew how to be successful in school, how to nail an essay. What I didn't know was how to make a living from my passion. In my gut I knew that school was my way of deferring that petrifying dilemma, the one where I make money by doing work that matters. That insight led me to launch the business I secretly dreamed of creating, the business that scared the living divine light out of me. As a direct result of that business, I began speaking more, writing more, risking more. I pushed the edges of my fear because, even when I wasn't actively remembering that Saturday afternoon, I knew that the only other choice was to shrink down. Something inside me had grown bigger that day, whether I was ready for it or not.

Failing Big

Of course, I increased my chance of failing significantly, too. And it wasn't always pretty. I "failed" at two versions of my business before I really stepped into the whole story, the big version that was the right business. Although I have had more Web site iterations than there are dress changes at a traditional Chinese wedding, I suspect that I'm not done in that area. I will continue to work toward the right online expression of my big work in the world, even if it means I have to start over – again.

I spent two solid years reaching out to the wrong clients, ones who didn't need or want my particular skills and gifts, but who were kind souls who *liked* me. I was simply too afraid to go after the ones that play bigger, the ones who really need what I have to offer. I was afraid they would not see my gifts. In fact, I was afraid that I had no gifts and that they would simply call me out on that fact. I was afraid I would learn, after all of this, that I was wrong about the ways I can change the world.

Guess what? That's not at all what happened. As soon as I stepped into my willingness to be great, to play big, to make the biggest difference I was capable of making in the world, I began to thrive—financially, spiritually, emotionally. Mentors I had put on pedestals began to ask me to collaborate with them, to help them from my areas of expertise. Clients I had wished for previously, but did not have the guts to attract, sought me out. I got e-mails from unexpected places asking me to speak, train and coach. Suddenly, my business was actually working.

It wasn't until I started playing bigger that I was able to create the business I wanted. The only way to do that was to be willing to do everything bigger, including fail.

Real Contribution

The good news, so far, is that the bigger game is a righteous one. It's scary sometimes, but I am radically clear that it is my job to step into real contribution in a big way. When I watch a client take the stage with ease, confident in their own version of real contribution, I am reminded how important it is that I survived that Saturday afternoon. I've got work to do. I've got a difference to make in the lives of my clients, my causes and my family.

So, I'll take real contribution over safety from failure any day. That I'm here, capable of making a meaningful difference in the world is amazing. That any of us gets this crazy cool opportunity to make our mark—make a difference, use our gifts to make this world better— is awesome.

I don't think about that Saturday afternoon very often. When I do, my heart still plummets into my gut and my insides feel like a washcloth being wrung out to dry. Not only did my life nearly end that day, but my baby girl was in that car with me, too. Despite the fact that nothing happened, the sheer horror of considering the alternative outcome from that speeding blue car was enough to absolutely and irrevocably change my life.

My uneventful near-death experience still lives quietly in the pocket behind my heart. I don't talk about it much. Yet it is one powerful little story for me. It encourages me to keep stepping up, even if it's scary. It reminds me that my chance to make this world a better place —for my kids, for their kids, for everyone—is now. Just. Only. Right. Now.

And I'm taking it. Head on. Full throttle. Big.

What about you? Are you ready to play bigger too? Because we need you out here.

Questions for Reflection

- Have you had the inkling that you might be playing smaller than is possible in your own life—either in work, relationships, family or otherwise? Maybe you aren't charging enough for your services? Maybe you take on too many tasks that you shouldn't be handling? Possibly you are avoiding an important conversation for fear of conflict? If so, name those small plays—and their counterparts, the ways you might play bigger in each of them.

- What would playing big look like for you overall? Even better, draw a picture of it. Or create a Vision Board.

- If you were to play bigger, what would it feel like for you, in your body, in your heart, and in your way of thinking about your life?

- What is one thing you could do today, even just a small thing, that would allow you to step into a bigger version of your life?

- What is stopping you from doing that one thing today—just today, just that one thing? Or is there anything stopping you?

About Michelle Barry Franco

Michelle Barry Franco, MA, CPC, spends a lot of time staring at her three daughters and husband, marveling at her amazing fortune. The rest of the time she helps passion-driven people change the world with their message. Michelle is the creator of **The Business You Came to Build** program, which guides authors, speakers, coaches and consultants through the process of building a business based on their passion. She is a popular speaker and published writer on topics from parenting to how to be less boring in business. Get cool free stuff on both of Michelle's websites listed below:

www.michellebarryfranco

www.mbfprofessionaldevelopment.com

Effortless Commitment

by Melanie McCloskey

Effortlessness happens

Trying to describe my connection to skiing is like trying to describe love: I can tell you all about how it fulfills me, but I can't describe fully why I am so passionate about it. How is it I happen to be effortlessly magnetized by this particular thing more than any of the other things I feel committed to in life? More than my career? More than yoga?

But I'm not going to talk about yoga yet. I'm going to keep telling you about skiing.

No matter how I feel, no matter what the conditions, I'm committed to skiing as many precious days of the winter as I possibly can. When the snow is good, I don't look for ways to dodge the early morning drive. I don't come up with excuses to stay inside my warm house. The more wild and blustery the weather, the more excited I get. Windstorms are heavenly. Whiteouts are bliss. Exhausted, long after others have retreated home on a deep powder day, you'll still find me wooed by one more untracked run. When I'm alone on the mountain, I often plop down in the snow to soak in the silence and peace provided by the white, blanketed forest. Completely absorbed in the moment, the rest of life is paused. I am 100 percent there, enjoying the interplay of snow conditions and varied terrain, mental focus and physical challenge. Skiing is the one thing that wins my devotion.

Much more than a sport to me, skiing triggers a state of mind that reaches my most authentic self. I identify with the four major pillars of my being, which are all at once challenged and touched by the beauty of this activity. **Spiritually**, engaging playfully in the natural elements renews me. **Emotionally**, I'm joyful and at peace. **Mentally**, I'm sharp and life comes into focus. **Physically**, I'm challenged and recharged. On the mountain, I am in my power. Regardless of conditions or my own performance that day, I get to experience my best self, perfectly balanced in the moment. I'm fed so deeply on all levels by this activity that it has become effortless for me to commit to heading to the mountains.

Change is inevitable

A few years ago, things took a turn when an unfortunate chain of events drastically changed my relationship with skiing and with my body as a whole. What followed was disorder and chaos so unfamiliar that it stopped me in my tracks. It started me on a journey of healing that required a deep commitment to change. As a person who had become accustomed to filling up others' cups before her own, this winding path of experiences unveiled a new awareness that ultimately brought me to a deep conviction for self love as the fastest avenue to growth. Thankfully, I dig growth.

Ignoring it doesn't make it go away

I hurt my back. Not just once, but multiple times over a few years. Not just slightly, but collectively, very seriously. All together, I experienced bulging discs and jammed facets, a sprained sacroiliac joint, endless strained muscles and out-of-nowhere spasming episodes. One winter, in the midst of on-and-off pain, a record early-season snowfall lured me to the mountains. I resisted the voices telling me to stay at home, enjoy a fireside cup of tea, and wait until I was in better shape and instead followed the siren song of the amazing powder. The hard days of skiing, combined with heavy snow shoveling, followed by a seemingly innocent slip on the ice set me back all of my progress. The pain was immobilizing, at times for days. Yet, it was still easier to ignore it and refuse to accept the hard road ahead. "It's no big deal", I told myself time and time again.

Life goes on

Consequently, life at the time of my back injury was full of uncertain transitions. My job, home, family and life path were all up for grabs. Rather than focus my energy on stabilizing my health, I put energy into figuring how to move my life forward. During those peaceful days on the mountain, I clearly knew my soul was guiding me on the path to becoming a personal coach but I was a long way from realizing that vision. Instead of working directly towards that goal, I was compelled to quit my stable job of three years to focus on a new career path. Thinking I should get secure employment, I worked on applications to do aid work overseas while researching going back to school. Needing income, I distracted myself with intense freelance projects for others. Rather than making calculated actions and committing to one path, I shot multiple darts figuring one would eventually hit the bull's eye.

At the same time, in order to remain flexible for whatever career choice I made, I became a chronic house sitter. Most of my life was in storage and I moved frequently. Without a steady job or home, my future was a blank slate.

During this time, it became easy to minimize my own health problems in comparison to the health issues of those around me. Various friends and family were dealing with cancer. My own mother was undergoing chemo and radiation treatment on the other side of the country. And to top it all off, my 16-year-old wonder dog had finally declined in health to the point that I had no choice but to help her pass on. It was the hardest thing a pet companion signs up for.

As certain as I was that things needed to change; my feelings of loss, fear and uncertainty paralyzed me. I wanted to be in action but found it was way easier to prioritize others before myself and to let go of what didn't work than commit to figuring out what would.

Embrace the unknown

Each of these transitions individually would have been difficult but bearable. All together at once, they took their toll. Physically, I was stiff and feared things were getting worse. I put off getting an

MRI, which could solidify my deepest fear: You are broken. Even my doctor's advice haunted me, "Only spend money on an MRI if you are open to surgery." She knew me so well: That's not the road I would take if there were any other options. So rather than getting expensive clarification, I embraced the unknown and took it one day at a time.

If you don't decide what's important, something else will

I was drawn back to skiing time and time again, but it became my nemesis instead of my freedom. My doctor told me to take it easy, but we both knew I would ski regardless. Needing a sanity fix when I could physically manage, I stubbornly went up the mountain. Seeking my old escape, skiing drew me, but I repeatedly left in frustration. My back's steady protest wouldn't allow me to relax. I quickly lost steam as my body was out of shape, stiff and guarded. With every turn I was afraid to make a wrong move. The experience of skiing had transformed from one of joy, excitement and ease to one of fear, frustration and yet again, loss.

Pain was constant – yet each day I wondered to what degree it would flare, and if I would be stuck in bed. **Mentally** I had no idea how to move forward. I questioned how my future would play out in my career and relationships. **Emotionally**, I spiraled in the victim mentality: "Why?" I was overcome with frustration and "stuckness", immobilized not just by my back, but by life and not knowing how to make it all better. I mourned the loss of physical and life freedom. **Spiritually**, I kept posing the question, "What am I supposed to learn from this experience?" I felt a separation from my body and the inability to stay present within it. The fear drove me to tears and I fought off despair. I felt unsupported. I felt stuck.

Eventually my body's pain signal became the straw that broke the camel's back. When getting in and out of my car became as challenging for me as skiing a beautiful, steep slope I finally woke up to the truth: This pain wasn't going away. Surgery or not, many things would need to change. Pain was just one piece of a complex web of issues causing me grief, and overcoming them wouldn't be an easy task. This is when I started to see the bigger picture. My energy couldn't go everywhere at once and I had to prioritize myself over my career, my home, and even others. I was in for a lot of hard work, the kind of work that involves serious change, a long-term commitment, and my undivided attention. I was afraid of that.

Losing the easy makes you face the hard

Ok, so about yoga. Like skiing, I've had a long-term affair with yoga. Like skiing, I have a deep connection with yoga and I know it supports me on all levels. Unlike skiing, it takes some serious negotiating with myself to make it happen with any regularity. It's hard to get myself on the mat. Being the drifter I am, my commitment level has always been fickle. The same goes for my personal practice of eating right for my body, journaling, meditating and so many other things. "If these things make me feel great and they are so good for me, why can't I be consistent? Why can't they be easy?"

Of course, as with any relationship, when the going gets tough you are reminded why they are in your life to begin with. I knew that yoga was the key. Everything life was throwing at me was too much for my brain to work through. Yoga was the key practice I could do to calm myself on all levels and at the same time gain physical strength.

Step up to the mat

With a deep acceptance of my situation, I had subconsciously become ready to face my physical, mental, emotional and spiritual fears. But if it was hard to commit to the mat before, that was nothing compared to now.

Now, tentatively stepping onto the mat, I discovered even there, **physically**, I was brittle; **mentally**, I felt weak; **emotionally**, I was scared; and **spiritually** I was completely disconnected. I openly shed tears in class. Before, yoga had been a safe retreat, now it was a battlefield. My out-of-control life had even shown up on the mat.

Rediscover your Authentic Self

Fear was everywhere, inside and out. I was ungrounded and uncertain. I had proven myself to be an inherently strong, determined, insightful person overcoming countless life challenges in the past. Where was that gal now? In moments of clarity, I recognized a need to build my strength on every level—physically, mentally, emotionally and spiritually. But my need for freedom in other parts of my life did not allow integrity with my body to be met and my need to remain optimistic did not allow me to express my authentic self.

Lucky for us, the body has an incredible ability to offer insight and heal itself. With this inherent resilience, we often only need to consciously allow ourselves the attention, space and energy to heal. As a coach, I generate a constant stream of questions seeking to help others overcome life's challenges and find peace. My curiosity about why people do what they do and how they can get better results is insatiable. So when it came to my own life challenges, I knew I wasn't asking myself the right questions.

Energy is a commodity

As a coach, I well know that life energy is a commodity. This valuable resource is often unconsciously spent on our daily tolerations. Fear, circumstance, stress, poor digestion, injuries or traumas, and worry for life's past or future are all tolerations we let drain our life force. When the majority of our unconscious energy is out to lunch, there is not enough in the here and now for mental clarity or physical healing.

My body had relentlessly shouted at me to stop and listen. Pestering was key. I needed to pull my energy from everywhere else and focus solely on my back. This meant saying no to skiing with a fragile body, but it also meant things like going to bed early and turning off all of those negative, worrisome thoughts about how my life should be different and the difficulties others around me were experiencing.

Stability, in both my back and my life, was the desired state. To get there, I needed to be objective about my situation. I needed to accept things in order for them to change. Knowing I could build core strength as well as mental clarity through yoga, I started to reach to it with more courage and regularity.

Embrace your inner warrior

Diving into the quiet of the yoga practice, I rediscovered my absolute favorite pose: Virabhadrasana II or Warrior II. Sinking in as you reach in all directions you are honoring the past and future, while being strongly grounded in the present. Energy flows in all directions, forward and back, out each arm, supported through your strong legs by the solid earth. Your back and head are drawn effortlessly towards the sky. A flow of energy emanates from your core, connecting with the flow felt from above, below, behind and forward and for a fleeting moment, you experience complete balance. You are both energetically held by the world and actively asserting yourself in it. Giving and receiving in perfect balance, you are claiming your space in the world and giving back with your connection to it. When you are strong, the power, flow and grace of this pose feels *effortless*.

One day I came upon the origin and meaning behind Virabhadrasana II. The story goes that in the warrior pose, you become a warrior against self-deception. It takes a presence of both mind and body to confront this ultimate source of suffering. When you are open to truth and self-love, you neutrally witness both your strengths and challenges. On the mat, this translates to caring for yourself, minding your alignment and not pushing too far outside your body's comfort. The trick is to allow the body to relax and stretch while holding the truth. Accepting you are perfect just the way you are, right here, right now. There is no desire or need for you to be different in any way. Being in the thick of the injury and my personal growth pains, it was a serendipitous aha moment.

In life, this witness to truth equates to having infinite compassion, loving yourself wholeheartedly, letting things unfold without judgment and walking in the world unguarded no matter what the situation. Feeling at ease with open vulnerability and solid grace. When you authentically care for yourself, you model courage and safety and, in turn, create a ripple effect, allowing others to be more authentic and loving. With truth and integrity in this pose, as in life, we experience ourselves as bright stars among many, expansive in space and time, accepting our beautiful imperfections that define our human experience and guide our path.

Don't should yourself

By letting go of all resistance in a yoga pose, we ask our body with compassion and curiosity, "What do you need to let go of? What is it you need to heal?" This detachment from how we "should" feel or the shape we "should" be in allows us a freedom from rigidity and control. With trust, as our bodies inevitably shift, we will accept it with curiosity, as a dance of love, rather than a war of resistance. As we let go in the moment to how our body "should" feel, we also invite this practice of letting go on a larger scale. As self-trust and acceptance grow, we fear our life, circumstances and personal suffering less. Through fostering this mindfulness, curiosity, self-love and acceptance, we allow ourselves to tap into our own rich inner-knowing and ultimately the guidance of the collective.

One thing at a time

Through the quiet lessons of yoga, and that poignant Warrior II, I realized the person who had stepped on the mat was not the authentic me. How could I be when I had been allowing myself to be overwhelmed by the perceived gravity of changes around me? While my body was trying to heal itself, I was focusing on everything but that, in effect, adding insult to injury. In avoiding my fears in one place, focusing on fearing the unknown, I was deceiving myself about what really mattered: the here and now, the back.

Ever so slowly, I started to gain strength. **Physically**, the back began to right itself with my new found core strength. **Mentally** experiencing progress, I knew I could heal. **Emotionally** I found a safe space to open and mourn and still celebrate small victories. **Spiritually**, I regained a trust with my entire being. I was able to connect again to my body and begin that empathetic dialogue. In a quiet place, a corner had been turned. Love overtook fear again. I saw my situation with objectivity and it was easy to be mindful and nurturing toward myself. Ever motivated to get my life on track and move forward, I realized it was to be a journey dictated by the process and I was along for the ride. I accepted that I had to change things one at a time. I accepted micro movements forward to be the quantum leaps I had hoped for. I had gotten to this place over time, so time and attention were needed to return to a state of grace.

Mindfulness: It's that easy

The dictionary defines mindful as attentive, aware or careful. To be mindful of the whole self includes being careful, aware and attentive to the physical, mental, emotional and spiritual parts of your being. I had felt by committing to a regular easy yoga practice I could build some muscle to support my core. I found through yoga that mindfulness was actually the key to that and more.

Shift happens

As things compassionately shifted on the inside, like a dance, the outside responded in kind. The helplessness I had felt was replaced with a renewed sense of trust and strength. I became open to new ways of being in the world and my outside reality did the same. As my back released its sense of "stuckness", life began to flow with a new ease. Instead of seeking the perfect work or taking jobs that drained me, I was recruited for work that fulfilled me and helped further my career path. My list of clients grew through word of mouth and my business built itself in a sustainable manner. Better living situations appeared. An amazing support system emerged when I came out of my protective shell. As I let go of the fear, I blossomed into a more conscious person allowing myself to be more supported than ever with both an internal and external trust. Amazingly, it took little effort.

One unfolding leads to another

Listening to my body was a quiet and intimate process. It was a conversation where I would look for signals and sense shifts when heading in the right direction. Yoga was one step, mindfulness another, each opening the next door. As I delved into my body with positive results it kept asking for more support and one thing led to another.

For years I had contemplated visiting a naturopath to work out digestive challenges and get tested for food intolerances, but I was, of course, stubborn and resistant to change. Health not being my priority at the time, I was out at a movie one night and mindlessly ate an entire bag of red licorice and washed it down with a beer. After a debilitating two-day migraine, I was finally able to pinpoint that a specific ingredient, red dye #5, was not my friend. Little did I know that beer wasn't either. This small insight fueled my curiosity. Friends had discovered through naturopaths what their bodies did or did not thrive on and it had a very positive impact on their quality of life. An enthusiastic advocate for natural healing, I had regularly utilized chiropractic, massage, acupuncture and energy work to physically balance myself. I knew digestion was the first line of defense and the source of our body's immunity, but stubborn as I am, I again thought it would work itself out or eventually I could figure it out on my own. Regardless, the time hadn't been right to accept the support until one random day it was. The migraines were too much on top of the back pain. I was in the midst of my healing process, what was one more little change?

In my two-hour introductory appointment the doctor passively mentioned, "Oh, you should stop having those back spasms now". Really?!? Years of ridiculously debilitating, painful, lay-me-out-for-a-day, random spasms are triggered by my unhappy gall bladder? Not to mention the migraines, slow digestion and systemic inflammation. Needless to say, from that day forward I steered clear of everything from food dyes to wheat, refined sugar, cow dairy, alcohol, caffeine, and all additives in order to feel better. I grew up with farming, had been a healthy vegetarian for 18 years, worked at holistic health clinics, studied nutrition and supplements and, if any average person could, I knew good food. The difference was I had overdone it on some things and I wasn't choosing the *right* good food to support my what my body was needing. I knew it... but hadn't been committed to it. Realizing the massive benefits, I put that stubborn streak to good use revamping my eating habits with serious commitment.

Trust feels better than trepidation

There is a delicate interplay between the four parts. Looking back, I wish I could say there was one Hollywood style aha moment when everything turned around, but it just doesn't work that way. It was a slow mindful shift on how I approached things, a deep attention to my body and taking one step after another in the right direction. As I regularly practiced yoga I rebuilt my core strength and started to carry myself with trust rather than trepidation. This new inner strength gave me the courage to listen deeper and take another step. On a roll, I sought out more healing to support the shift. With the naturopath I completely revamped my diet to support healing and supplemented the nutrients my body was craving.

Coaching works

Like any coach worth their salt, I know to take my own medicine. I regularly received coaching support while on this journey. As time went on, I grew better able to neutrally reflect on my situation and self-corrected my wayward path more and more quickly. When exploring challenges through the co-creative process of life coaching, we pinpoint a person's needs, and like my experience with yoga, create a safe space for the whole person to expand and explore resolutions. When the body and spirit are truly able to trust that they are supported, the person as a whole is able to let their guard down, release answers and enable forward movement. I feel honored to have witnessed many beautiful aha moments when clients open to their authentic selves and find clarity. As I witnessed the power of my own attentiveness to the spiritual, emotional, mental and physical parts of the self, I was better able to reflect on clear shifts happening in others through the language of the different parts.

I recognized through mindfulness that health is a constant conversation. *Physically*, I ask daily, "Will this food or action feel good to my body? Will this trigger a stress response or support me to thrive?" *Mentally* I take breaks more often and ask myself, "What's the outcome I want here?" and notice when I'm unproductively worrying. *Emotionally*, I keep myself in check by compassionately questioning when feeling off-kilter "What need is not being met right now?" *Spiritually*, I notice when I lack connection to nature, myself or my tribe and take steps to get back in tune or just be with the noticing. Putting trust in a more fine-tuned awareness, my stubborn do-it-yourself sensibility melted a bit. I listened with new interest to my previously hard-to-discern intuitive voice. It grew loud and clear as I became used to trusting it. When internally guided, I sought support of my tribe for coaching, healing and connection.

The result? So much. I effortlessly receive what I truly need. With my diet and body awareness changes, I have much less pain, clearer thinking and a happier outlook on life, and even lost twenty pounds without noticing. Friends and strangers comment on my vibrancy, life feels more abundant and I have faith in the unfolding of things.

Even the most challenging terrain is a gateway to joy

Oddly, one of the best results of the journey with my back is witnessing how it played out in the mountains. Yes, I returned with a new level of strength having learned to better use my core and as a bonus became an even stronger skier. Even better though, I have a different awareness, empathy and respect for myself as a whole. This new way of holding myself actually created a whole new connection with the mountains as well as with myself. Now, while mindfully focused on core strength and the task at hand, I notice my life awareness, appreciation and creativity expand exponentially. Just being present on the mountain I sink into the enjoyment of feeling my body as it turns the edge of the ski to flow gracefully down the fall line, the steep lines again becoming my friends to revisit again and again. With these friends, even the most challenging terrain is a gateway to joy. And being mindful, I take these seeds of joy, creativity and awareness that the mountains offer home to spill into the rest of life.

Love is always the answer

While I have always been effortlessly committed to skiing, my injury taught me that effortless commitment is possible in all areas of life, even yoga. Having dissolved resistance, pain and uncertainty, I can similarly tap into the joy I experience on the mountain in the rest of life. I'm a warrior against self-deception. I now get to experience moments of complete mindfulness in action. Rather than procrastinate and avoid the challenging questions out of fear, I'm more able to be present and focused with a clear mind and pure heart. With awareness of the strength I offer by staying in balance with the four parts of myself, I prioritize this steadiness while being effortlessly committed to the amazing people I get to serve. Life is a dance between priorities rather than a struggle. Some days this focus is my business. Some days, it's my garden. Some days it's self-care. Some days it's definitely skiing.

I gotta run, the snowy trees are calling me and I'm ready to take in the next lessons.

Life Lessons:

Spiritual, Emotional, Mental and Physical

By compassionately seeking to keep the four pillars of ourselves equally weighted, the commitment to your life purpose becomes effortless.

Curiosity, compassion and courage

Facing life with curiosity, compassion and courage is paramount to creating change. Over time, vulnerably approaching your challenges with these three values can break down every self-imposed barrier in your way.

Love

Being courageous enough to make changes based on treating your body with love and respect has a snowball effect on your life. As if by magic, that love and respect is returned to you from your outer world and circumstances.

Questions for Reflection

- What does it mean for you to be mindful? What activity brings you completely present and engages your body on all levels?

- What do you do to keep your balance between inner power and wisdom and being supported by the outer world?

- How much of your life energy is available to you in this very moment? How much is delicately balancing tolerations like worry, fear, physical and mental stress? How would life be different if you reclaimed your life source?

- What would shift if you responded to your challenges with love instead of fear?

About Melanie McCloskey

Melanie is a certified professional coach, consultant and Reiki Master. She considers herself inherently lazy and uncommitted and loves to study what makes things effortless. As a coach, Melanie works like a lighthouse guiding clients around their imagined rocks. She encourages people to listen deeply and challenge their beliefs until they find their own truths. Melanie's superpower is helping people hone in on what matters most while expanding their expectations and leveraging their essential nature. Certified in Whole Person Design Coaching, she utilizes a holistic, heart-centered approach as well as the practice of Compassionate Communication and positive emotions. She realizes she might work her way out of a job by helping her clients uncover their inner fire, and that's OK.

Never too far from her passion for telemark skiing and nature, Melanie makes her home on fertile ground between two snow-capped peaks in the abundant Columbia River Gorge.

www.melaniemccloskey.com

Our next story is from one of our graduates who is applying Whole Person coaching inside of corporations to develop leaders and teams. Although, the bulk of the stories inside this book are personal, we felt that Mary's work demonstrates the power of coaching both personally and professionally.

Put Your Mask On First

by Mary Sommerset

When times are good it's difficult to slow down and take a look around. Many companies missed the signs of the looming recession of 2008. Investment firms with integrity stopped making investments and began to "circle the wagons" to protect investors. This is a story of one such company that is in the process of transforming itself into a leaner, more agile firm, willing and able to adapt to new market trends.

In the two years that followed the crash they licked their wounds, laid people off and waited. Naturally, morale was at an all-time low among the survivors. I began coaching the executive team towards the end of 2010. Our goal was to determine if we had the "right people on the bus" and in the right seats. Further, the goal was to improve meetings, increase communication, and foster transparency. Emotions ran high. There was division in the company, with individuals aligning with different leaders. Mistrust of each other was rampant.

In addition, this had been a top down organization; now two of the three principals wanted to plan for retirement. For a plan to be effective, the new leaders had to be identified and groomed. A three-year succession plan was started. The difficulties entrepreneurs have turning over their companies to new leadership is legendary. These company leaders were no exception. Age does matter, however, and as the CEO was in his seventies, it was believed that he really did want to leave the day-to-day leadership of his company.

Still it was one step forward and two steps back. This was also due to a generational divide in work ethics. Instilling a sense of urgency among all players was a key role for me as a coach. This approach to urgency acted as a unifier in getting everyone to agree to the new direction. As trust began to develop we looked at the necessary activities for moving forward.

First, make sure we have the right people on the bus. What often happens during downturns and subsequent downtimes is the development of a culture of blame. This had affected two employees to the detriment of themselves and the team. Coaching is a client-driven activity. Asking insightful questions to elicit the truth from a person can allow that person to see for himself the path to take. I was fortunate to be able to coach one of the two people through the process, which led to an amicable parting of ways. The lesson learned here is that we need to look at ourselves first and what we want rather than blaming someone else for our pain.

Hiring two new, more enthusiastic players contributed to the transformation. It also shone a light on the people who remained. An understanding grew that everyone who was still there both deserved and wanted be there. Identifying a new executive team came with promises of profit sharing. Keeping those promises in the face of lawsuits, partner agreements, and more, proved difficult at first, largely due to misunderstandings between the current and new executive teams. Mistrust began to rise again. Coaching each team to change perspective to include the other proved helpful.

Profit sharing is still a work in progress, as it is often difficult for principals to change the financial picture, making it potentially less beneficial for themselves and more beneficial for the company as a whole. Profit sharing represents a shift in culture. Significant work with belief systems is a big part of the coaching work. Lessons learned thus far involve how each individual values the firm and the opportunity. And how giving feedback in a sensitive manner is essential.

With the right people in the right seats, the next step was to develop the new team into leaders who could operate effectively within two to three years, the expected time frame for retirement. This required leadership development. My background in both start-ups and global software companies, and participation in a wide variety of leadership workshops, proved extremely helpful in coaching the new team to develop as strong leaders.

It also became clear that strategic partnerships could benefit the firm during this transition. Again, coaching was a valuable ingredient to both preparing the new partner and allowing the client to express fears and desires prior to making the deal. Active listening to both parties in the partnership was critical.

It has been said that in any given conversation there are actually at least six conversations happening. The first person speaking is telling his story. He believes he is telling the truth. He also believes it is understood. The listener in this case hears what the person is saying but may question the truth or validity. He then applies his own filters to come to an understanding not necessarily intended by the first speaker. If questions are not asked to clarify the meaning of a statement, the entire communication between partners can be derailed.

There are also times when a communication may be couched in somewhat vague terms in order to "protect' the speaker from directly exposing his thoughts to criticism. Again, the lesson learned here is to ask courageous questions. Of course how the question is asked is paramount to a successful conclusion. Understanding and appreciating the vulnerable nature of negotiating strategic partnerships is a necessary umbrella covering the partner communications.

Discretion of the coach is imperative for success. In order to build trust in an organization with poor internal communication, I listened empathetically and provided feedback to tease out the real issues. Once the trust was established, real fears from each of the executive team were explored. I was then able to take the impersonal part of the fear and present it to the president and CEO in a way they each could hear it. This was not always easy. My staying neutral and not taking his reaction personally allowed the client to do the same. The team now had the information out in the open and could make progressive plans.

With the background of this client and some of the basic needs in improving communication understood, let's look at three specific areas: 1. Leadership development of the new team 2. Succession planning for the chairman/CEO, and 3. First phase of strategic partnership development.

Leadership Development

The president of the company, a long time principal, was being groomed for the CEO role. Being the number two guy is very different from "being the man." Learning how to step up to the number one position requires taking responsibility for one's decisions. It also includes developing management skills to build the necessary team to support the new president.

For this process, I worked directly with each of the three executives expected to take over when the principals retire. Together they have the combined strength to successfully execute the mission. The president is a master at sourcing and making deals, a very "present moment" type job. One of the executive vice president's roles, with his numbers background and attention to detail, is as the chief operations officer. The other executive vice president is a big picture person and an excellent motivator and mentor to people. He, like his colleagues, has a deep knowledge of the business.

It was fair to say in the beginning, that these three individuals worked more autonomously than as a team. Although their individual strengths were considerable, they had previously worked in an environment where the CEO called the shots. In such a situation it is easy for "water cooler talk" to spread. Underlying resentments of how things work, when talent has a minimal outlet, can develop into low morale.

When working with a group of leaders, it is the coach's role to bring out each individual's strengths. It is important to communicate the non- personal information important to the company reaching its goal in such a way that people feel fulfilled and supported.

Through the coaching process, each of these leaders were able to express their fears, which previously had been misunderstood by their partners creating mistrust. Helping the new executive team face this mistrust was difficult, yet provided the most poignant moments relevant in successfully developing the new team.

Several of the team members wanted to develop interpersonal skills. I recommended *The Four Agreements* by Don Miguel Ruiz. He tells us: Be impeccable with your word; Don't take things personally; Don't make assumptions; Always do your best. It is remarkable how often our grievances can be traced back to one or more of these agreements.

Next I want to work on the strengths of each person, using *Strength Finders 2.0* by Tom Rath. As we build the team, it will be very helpful to understand each leader's strengths and the strengths of the team. That will also help them identify what strengths may be missing and who else may need to be added to the team. The lesson learned here is that strengths trump weaknesses. Shifting the culture from blame to proactive effort requires a new lens for seeing others. It also allows a budding leader to accept that another person may be better suited to a particular task, which makes it possible for him to let go of some control. It also allows the leader to feel good about his strengths and admire those of his colleague, rather than threatened. All three members, and the CFO on the new executive team are excited about this approach.

Succession Planning

The first step in succession planning is making the commitment. This is a very personal decision. In this case, the chairman/CEO had several options: 1) sell the company as is; 2) develop a new executive team to take over; 3) shut the company down and walk away. The market eliminated choice number one. The chairman decided to develop a new executive team. That decision inspired more participation in how best to increase revenues.

How did he make the decision? Coaching an executive who created his company from the ground up to even think of succession planning can be difficult. Working with the personal goals of the chairman, in this case, was the winning solution. I asked him about his bigger "why?" He is well known in his community for raising large amounts of funds for charities and the arts. He wanted to leave an ongoing entity for his sons and daughter and grandchildren to take pride in. This was consistent with his community legacy.

The next step following the commitment was to develop a succession plan. In addition to these meetings, the new executive team was invited to participate in growth and planning meetings. In the beginning, this process was not pretty. Succession planning may be one of the more challenging undertakings, however, the benefits of such planning can be tremendous. As the players were not communicating well with each other, my role was to draw out of each player "what would make it better". I was able to take out any personal references then convey the business idea to each member of the team in turn.

Over time this process built trust within the team and with me. We are now engaged in the next steps of succession planning, assessment of the current employees and developing the action plan for execution.

The lesson learned here is to not expect a smooth march forward to a perfect succession plan. By its nature, succession planning requires everyone to change: To change how they see themselves and others and to change beliefs that may have served them well in the past but are no longer serving anyone.

Strategic Partnerships

As the new executive team learned skills for speaking up and began to trust in the succession plan, it became possible to entertain a strategic partnership to fully assess their company's position in the private equity market and determine if a joint venture could bring new investors into the fold.

At the assessment presentation by the potential partner, each of the new executives played a key role. Everyone listened to one another and asked many questions. Each member of the team came prepared and played to his own strengths. For the first time, the new executive team acted like a team. The chairman was pleased to see his team in action. The lesson learned here is to be patient. Coaching requires courageous questions; and it also requires consistent positive energy. For months, I had been encouraging each member of the team to realize his potential. Because of the trust we had established, each one began to believe in the possibilities and to reach for his goal.

In conclusion, I am very grateful for the opportunity to coach these bright and talented men. I have grown in the process. Building trust may be the single most important thing about successful coaching. And lack of effective internal communication may be the biggest problem facing companies today. With fast-paced, fragmented lives and multiple communication vehicles, few people in business feel they can take the time for the active listening a coach provides. Those that do have a greater likelihood of success.

Questions for Reflection

- What is your 'Why" for succeeding in business?

- Are you playing to your strengths?

- Are you making assumptions or taking things personally?

About Mary Sommerset

Mary Sommerset, CPC is a certified professional coach who promotes positive change with significant results as she works with individuals, business owners, entrepreneurs, executives, and managers. Mary is drawn to coaching as it focuses on the present and moving forward. Coaching is not therapy; there is relatively no work on the past. In coaching, Mary helps people shed unwanted, unproductive thoughts and behaviors and infuse themselves with optimism; Mary encourages surrendering the past and embracing the present.

Employing an engaging interactive approach, Mary motivates individuals and organizations to take on fresh perspectives; to shift the way they see, hear and think about the work they do. The end result... new solutions to old problems as the people and their business developed new skills and were able to let go of the past as they became happier, more focused; leading healthier lives; directing businesses and individuals to a brighter future.

Mary's knowledgeable yet playful presentations captivate her spectators with a distinctive style. Weaving real life experiences with proven techniques, she serves as a skillful guide over, around and through debilitating barriers and onto paths with richer, more rewarding prospects.

www.clearstreamcoaching.com

Hold Fast
to your,
B-side

by Richard Gear

Hold Fast to Your B-side is about celebrating both your ups and downs (the B-side of your own life's record.) As I believe it is both the good and the bad experiences that make your life interesting, dynamic, and totally awesome.

As a life coach, I challenge my clients to live with an "outlaw spirit," blaze nontraditional trails, explore risks as new adventures, and create life changes by following heart-based decisions. This is my story that led me to becoming a change agent and champion of those ready to find and release their inner outlaw...

For almost two decades I've been using the rich and highly expressionistic medium of tattooing as to illustrate the web of my life stories. My tattoos have had hard-traveling hootenannies. They have stories to tell. For me, my tattoos sing the color of my soul.

The first tattoo I got was in a biker-type shop in the Midwest where the head tattooer looked like Santa Claus's evil twin. It was then a rough part of town, and the street was not a safe place to be at that time. The guy behind the counter said, "If you don't like the way the tattoo comes out, you can always spray oven cleaner on it and burn it off!" That was old-school customer service. No lilies on the counter.

No hipsters in the shop. Just badass, old-school tattoos: panthers, eagles, skulls with daggers, and WWII bomber-style pinups.

I was afraid to go in. It felt like the kind of place where "bad shit" could happen, a place where you'd never see the light of day again. This first tattoo was just the beginning as many more were to come.

One empty night in Denver in the late 1990s, I was feeling restless and drove out to get my Rocky Mountain high—a caffeine fix. As I cruised down the creepy crawly concrete of East Colfax Boulevard, I cranked up 16 Horsepower's *Sackcloth 'n' Ashes* album. Their "Nick Cave meets Wood Guthrie" dirges propelled me all the way to Colby, Kansas. I pondered the meaning of life at 3:00 a.m. next to a 7-11 store. Unsuccessful at channeling any pearls of wisdom from the tumbleweed blowing by, I drove back to Denver the same night. It was a sign that my eight-year life in Denver was over. It was time to go explore and determine if the rumors I'd heard—that the Earth was not flat—were true. I packed my car full of all my possessions and hurtled off to explore the wilds of Portland, Oregon.

I was to spend my next decade in this city living amongst the undulating pines and dark emerald raindrops. I knew I was home when I received my first thumbs up from a native Oregonian while caught in the rain and not whining about it. By this time it was evident the webbing had spread to my toes — I had become one with the raindrop and had fully embraced Stumptown.

Portland has an insane number of coffee shops, 600 food carts, a huge bicyclist population, lots of excellent tattoo shops, the most strip clubs of any state in the nation, and a grip of tasty donut shops. This mad combination sings loudly to the Northwestern outlaw spirit. The town motto is *Keep Portland Weird!* And even though it's rapidly changing, parts of Portland still have that grungy 1970s *Drugstore Cowboy* feel that made me fall in love with it ten years ago.

Portland has many powerhouse, world-class tattoo shops. Living there, you get spoiled rotten by all of your ink options. Virtually every neighborhood has a couple of great shops with virtually any ink style available. I believe Portland once got voted the Fifth Most Tattooed City in America, and it's true: Go to the supermarket and you are sure to find someone with ink.

Portland is refreshing in that being heavily tattooed is a moot issue and not a barrier to employment. My favorite comment from a Portlander was an inquiry: "How are you going to get a good job *without* tattoos?" I was reminded of the supportive nature of this town during a recent trip across the country, where I found myself the object of many eyes, entrenched in observing my canvas. People are always shocked to find out I have a master's degree in social work.

After being bludgeoned by many Portland winters, I had an epiphany: I could take a road trip to California to escape the relentless sheets of rain and newts flying out of the sky. Some people take vacations, go play golf and drink Arnold Palmers at the country club. I prefer taking spontaneous road trips to get tattooed and explore small, hole-in-the-wall dives. It's just what I do; it's part of my B-side. The outlaw nebula fun house speaks more to my authentic self. You're not supposed to walk behind the mirrors, but I do every day.

The tattoos I get on my various trips have left me with markers in time that become living photos albums, celebrating my travels and outlaw spirit. Want to see who I am? Look at my *body* of work.

At some point, I planned what would become an annual pilgrimage to Santa Cruz. The drive out of Portland leads to Highway 101, which connects to Highway 1. This is probably the most magical drive I've found. The highway snakes along the breathtaking Pacific coastline—Northern California's old growth redwoods, the Mendocino valley, ocean-salt air blowing through your car window—and ends near San Francisco. Due to progressive action, the coastline has remained undeveloped, which is a rare happening in the modern real estate vortex. I think I was originally planning to stay in San Francisco but took a look at the hotel prices, almost ran over a huge dude on a motorcycle who rightly screamed some pretty awesome insults at me, and hit Bay Bridge traffic at rush hour. I thought, *Let's head south*. After all, I was trying to get away from all the stress of being a mental health crises counselor (it should be noted I was a biscuit shy of a visit to the state hospital myself). *F' this*! I thought. *This doesn't feel like a vacation*! Cue soundtrack to yuppie tragedies in E minor.

Let's skip ahead before this becomes a crappy travel guide. Fast forward through massive amounts of 7-Eleven nachos, junk food, exceptionally tasty truck-stop coffee, an 11-hour drive speaking in tongues about how the fourth dimension changed my life, glowing eyes from all the candy dye flowing through my system, and finally I arrive in Santa Cruz. I think I remember arriving just before 5:00 p.m. on

Friday. One of my first memories in Santa Cruz was driving around looking for a cheap motel. Turning onto a small side street, I came upon a dude in an epic *Munsters*-looking Rat Rod just "busting out" massive donuts in the middle of the street! He had a big beard and a huge grin on his face. "How f'ing awesome!" I thought.

I putzed around Santa Cruz until I found a motel right next to a liquor store, which always means you're in for some quality "parking lot 3:00 a.m. Creature Feature presents *When Blind Drunk Werewolves Attack!*" sponsored by Olde English 40-ounce malt liquor. I checked in immediately and worked on regrouping my frontal lobe back to pre-eleven-hour-road-trip functionality.

I was thinking about getting a tattoo, so I called up O'Reilly's Tattoo parlor. The owner, Robert Klem, just had a cancellation ... Bam! I'll take it. It was pretty awesome because the tattoo was going to be the next day, May 8th, my birthday. Hell, yeah! I didn't know what I was going to get, so Klem told me to just leave a brief description on his shop machine of what I wanted and he would draw it up in the morning.

Generally, I appreciate the old style "walk-in" tattoos. I like to just pick an image from the old flash on the shop wall, or an image the tattoo artist thinks might look good in the area. I am not a firm believer that every tattoo has to have some dramatic Greek tragedy connected to it or even "to be of a profound life event." Picking some flash from the early tattoo masters honors the foundation of tattooing and connects you to some of its godfathers. In the early days of tattooing, these timeless tattoo images made it across the equator and back on the weather-beaten bodies of tough-as-nails sailors. They will definitely travel well and are built to last. I forgot who said it, but tattoos shouldn't look like a peacock in blender! Sometimes a tattoo can just be a badass piece of art that you get to travel with the rest of your life.

I called the shop and left a brief message: Antique lock. Done ... five-second message. That night I had a nice stroll on West Cliff Drive, listening to the waves roll in and out, and contemplating the eve of getting one year closer to being an old man with pants up to my ribs, sitting on the porch with pile of crushed PBR cans to throw at kids, yelling, "Get out of my yard, kids!"

Now having a morning tattoo is a little like Christmas—you're very excited to get the day rolling! I arrived to see O'Reilly's Tattoo parlor for the first time around 11:00 a.m.—a clean-looking house on Mission Street, nice porch, no neon sign. I walked in and met Klem for the first time. Klem was a friendly, likeable gentleman covered in tattoos with that certain California flair (i.e., He didn't look like the typical Northwest hipster bike messenger or grunger type). The shop entrance had a very cool, open feel to it and some amazing artwork: a beautiful Chris Conn painting, a skateboard with zombie artwork, and awesome, traditional old-school American flash. Klem handed me a drawing of a beautiful antique lock with a key and one rose. "A lock's got to have a key," he said. I agreed and we decided the back of the triceps was a good spot.

The way O'Reilly's Tattoo parlor is broken up, it feels like you're getting tattooed in a house—it just feels right and comfortable. The weather in Santa Cruz was around 75 degrees that day, which does not suck for a Portlander. Coming out of rainy, dark Portland into California sunshine left me grinning like a fool. Klem took me to one of the back rooms, and we locked and loaded on a good palm-size lock, key and rose tattoo. I think Klem may have asked if there were any colors I wanted. When a tattoo artist asks me this question, I usually shut up and explain that I can't draw my thumbnail! I prefer to trust the artist to take care of business.

When the dust settled after about two hours, I got a look at the whole piece and it blew me away! Some really cool details in the lock and key. It had a great old-time feel contrasted with an orange burst coming out of the top of the lock with little red lines in it, and a killer, old-school rose with unique twists that made it his own. This was one badass tattoo ... I was super stoked! Many years later the tattoo still looks like it could have been done yesterday. In my book, it's the best birthday gift one could get.

I would come back for two more tattoos from Klem over the years—a diamond with wings (an apology to my mom for losing her wedding ring when I was five) and some cool, Cali-style script right beneath his lock that reads "Hope". Sometimes hope is like turning into a skid; it rights your path every time.

Remembering back to the early 1990s, when I lived in Denver, Colorado, and I became very involved with homeless youth, starting as a volunteer and finally becoming a counselor. After doing some outreach work on the rough streets of Colfax Boulevard, I became very aware of the myriad of risks faced by homeless youth.

After years of working with at-risk teens and homeless youth, I looked in the mirror one day and realized … whoa … I could do something different with my master's degree. I thought about going back to being a mixologist in a bar with black velvet paintings of unicorns and Elvis, serving whiskey neats … or maybe a new direction?

Coming out of graduate school and being more focused on outreach jobs in the community, I never would have believed I would jet land into a job with a headset and be tethered to a phone! I ended up working for a top behavioral health organization that provides 24-hour intake, assessment, crisis response and triage over the phone. Basically, I worked as a crisis phone counselor for eight years. In that time I talked to thousands of people from very different socio-economic backgrounds, cultural backgrounds and age demographics. It was a very challenging and rewarding job due to the diverse clinical situations I assisted clients with every day. The crew of counselors who work there are a magical group of folks. They are as tough as nails and care deeply about people they will never meet.

Incoming calls varied from general angst, marital problems, financial stress, drug and alcohol addictions, and substance abuse, to homicidal or suicidal thoughts. In fact, a large number of the calls were related to individuals who had thoughts of suicide. Sometimes you had to dispatch the police to ensure a caller did not harm themselves. The calls came from all over the U.S., Canada and once, from the UK. Due to the high volume of calls, I developed the skills to empathize and rapidly build rapport to access how best to assist the caller and ensure their safety. After eight years I decided to put the phone down and transition to life coaching.

I gained certain insights from this unique work experience and felt it might be beneficial to share my knowledge. Any worker who does first-responder type crisis work gets to see people in a very challenging corner. One thing I've come to realize is that massive positive movement in one's life can come from pushing out of the darkest corners. I don't know where I first heard the Chinese phrase "Danger equals opportunity," but it really crystallizes the unique perspective that can arise from surviving deep waters. People have a resiliency that is amazing. After a certain breaking point, people decide *enough* … and they make intentional choices to put themselves back in control of their lives. Sometimes just a small step has a profound ripple effect.

My favorite phrase related to grounding yourself in the perpetual eye of the storm is *hold fast*. Apparently, sailors would yell out, "Hold fast!" when in rough seas. I tend to be a very visual person, and that image of a sailor yelling that out with conviction, determination and intestinal fortitude is very powerful to me. The vision of getting through a very rough moment, and to believe it in your bones, is a conviction that can't be broken.

I felt honored to be there for the people who had the deep courage to reach out and call that crisis line. You may never hear from these folks again – that's the nature of the gig – but it's important to get that person to recognize it's time to sit down with someone and talk about tackling the problems in their life. That's a simplified version of a complex matrix, and sometimes a picture holds more weight than twenty-five-cent words! I didn't plan to get a tattoo of a phone with wings to mark that experience, but that's what I ended up with.

It was winter 2006 whilst on another jailbreak dash from Portland to Santa Cruz; I lucked out, and Adam Barton at O'Reilly's had a cancellation. I met Adam and discussed getting an antique phone with wings. I was super stoked to get a tattoo from Adam; I had been blown away by his tattoos for years. He has a unique style, and I'll just say his tattooing is off the grid. Adam is one of the tattooers who set the watermark for innovation. To be honest, I was a little nervous after talking with Adam about the tattoo ... "Did I just book a phone with wings tattoo? What the f' was I thinking!"

I met with Adam the day before the tattoo, and he said he wanted redraw the 1901 phone I had picked out to make it a little more dynamic. "I'm on board for sure," says the man with zero artistic chops. Adam's redraw was awesome. It already had a great antique feel, but he added a little motion to the phone cradle so it looked like it was ringing. The phone had amazing wings and some art nouveau adornments organically flowing off its base. This was going to be one badass half sleeve.

Adam cranked up some killer death-metal tunes and laid down the stencil, which went from my deltoid to the outside of my bicep. I don't remember exactly how long the black work and shading took, but it was more than two hours. The amount of detail and complexity of the tattoo blew me away. Adam asked me if I wanted to finish the tattoo or come back for another session ... I opted for finishing the tattoo. When

I saw all the colors Adam was putting down to prepare for the final leg of the tattoo, I got really excited: blues, oranges, reds, greens, and on and on … When the whole tattoo was finally completed and cleaned off—maybe four hours or more—I was incredibly excited. The tattoo was crazy beautiful, dynamic and had some really cool movement to it.

I couldn't believe how everything he tattooed came together. All the colors were jaw dropping in combination. Somehow, Adam captured the feeling by making a phone with wings appear triumphant. How the hell do you do that? The fact that he captured celebrating my crisis mental health work was really important to me and a huge gift. It let me acknowledge that part of my life and the courageous people who fought through tough times. It also allowed me to move toward closing a chapter of my own life. The fact that his tattoo released all that is a testament to the alchemy tattooing can conjure. Adam must have put some "come back dust" in the tattoo ink, because I would *come back* two more times to get more work. When I moved back to the East Coast, I brought my own O'Reilly's museum exhibit, minus the soap-smelling, stern top hats and desert-dry martinis!

What does all this mean? Bad travelogs should be put out of their misery before they put people to sleep? Ink and bold, positive actions both stand the test of time? I really don't know … but I do know that I still have all my tattoos. They've traveled to southern Africa, driven 130 miles per hour down an old country road, swam in freezing Pacific Ocean waters, shared stories with strangers I never would have met … and they're going down in a pine box with me. I also know that the hardest parts of your life— the parts you're avoiding—may be the biggest "root systems" you have. When I work with life-coaching clients via HoldFast Life Coaching, I try to get them to see that the parts of life they're the most frustrated with will be their road map to a new life. If you don't have any stories to tell, fear has become a "box and one" defense, trapping your heart from green-lighting your dreams. Perhaps the most powerful words of wisdom I've come upon were written by literary juggernaut Henry Rollins, one of my favorite spoken-word performers, musicians and all-around elemental force. An interviewer asked Henry a fairly heaving-hitting question about how he had turned his life around. His reply: "One morning I woke up and decided to become totally awesome." Other folks quote Gandhi … I quote Henry!

I want to thank all the tattoo artists that have done work on me over the years. Your tattoos are a gift that keep growing with me wherever I roam. I also want to thank those folks I'll never meet, those bold people I talked to over an eight-year period on the crisis line. I hope they're holding fast because, like Fats Waller used to say, "sometimes you got to waltz a rhumba."

Questions for reflection:

- How often do you embrace your inner outlaw?

- What piece of artwork could you hang on the wall that would remind you to hold fast to your dreams?

- What are 5 steps you could take immediately that would propel you into your new life?

About Richard Gear

Richard Gear, is not your average life coach. If you're looking for flowers and rainbows, you'll need to look elsewhere. Richard Gear is here to help you channel your inner outlaw, not your inner child. So if you're looking for less frou frou and more action, Richard Gear is the man with the plan.

But Richard is not all fun and games. He's a pro, too. He holds a masters in social work from the University of Denver and received his certification in Life Coaching from the Baraka Institute. After working as both private practice therapist and crisis mental health counselor, he has now chosen to focus on life coaching. Having lived all around the world and encountered his fair share of adventures, this tattoo-loving cyclist seeks to help his clients make proactive changes, not just sit around waiting for a light bulb moment.

As a life coach with HoldFast Life Coaching, Richard enjoys helping folks with diverse life challenges. Three founding principles frame the body of his work: Hold fast to your dreams; Honor your B-side (your inner outlaw, not your inner child); and Fortune favors the bold!

When he's not busy helping people create dynamic and full lives, he can be found driving around in his 1963 Chevy Impala listening to Slim Cessna and Motorhead. The best part? He has good teeth. Despite his British parents.

www.HoldFastLC.com

the Heart & Mind
Relationship:
FINDING YOUR INNER BALANCE

by Veronica Bishop

The words 'heart' and 'mind' hold many strong connotations for us all. I'm particularly fond of the way the French translate heart and mind to "l'amour et la raison" or "love and reason". Here, the heart is named after one of the most powerful feelings imaginable – love. (The French word for the organ itself is an altogether different word: 'une coeur'.) According to the French, the heart dictates emotion, feeling and need, and the mind promotes thought, reason and logic. Together they hold the space of higher awareness; who we are and who we wish to be can be found within these two sacred places, under the right circumstances. The heart and mind can function extremely well together, like partners working in sync: one guides the other. When our mind is in overdrive, the heart has the power to expand and guide us through troubled thoughts. And when the heart is burdened with sadness or despair, the mind can swoop in and get things organized, releasing us from the spirals of emotion.

But what happens when these two forces collide in conflict or distrust? What to do when the mind is tugging one way and the heart is pulling another, like two children fighting for ownership of the self? The heart wants and the head needs. "I want a new job, I want to move, I want a new partner", says the heart. "I need security, I need money, I need love", says the mind. When this occurs, the balance of power can become disproportionate, and eventually one part dominates the other. In this scenario, either the mind wins, or the heart wins. Although initially this resolution can feel rewarding and productive because one side has taken precedence over the other, eventually we may begin to feel 'stuck' or unbalanced, as though something is out of sync. Over time, some of us may begin to ask ourselves questions such as: "What is missing in my life?"

For me, this question has the potential to quickly unlock Pandora's Box. I could spend hours wading through my own fear and doubt, longing for something and asking myself: "What's wrong with me? What don't I have? Where did I make a wrong turn?" These thoughts can be all consuming, further contributing to a loss of balance and objectivity. This negative line of thinking does not illuminate the real problem: the divergence of the heart and mind partnership. When one drowns out the other, we lose our clarity and balance. Some of us are able to sense this even as it is occurring, while for others, the realization arrives slowly. How can we regain our equilibrium when the heart and mind are experiencing extreme marked discord?

The solution lies not within the answers to these questions, but within the questions themselves. As coaches, we learn to ask powerful, non-leading questions. As human beings, speaking to our selves, this is much easier said than done. But what if we could learn to shift the line of questioning within ourselves away from: "What am I missing?" and towards: "What do I have?" What if the answer lies not in trying to identify a *loss* of something, but seeing what is already there – hidden away?

When we ask questions based on what does not exist, how would we ever find the answers?

How would it feel if, in moments of deep uncertainty, I looked not to the negative thoughts and feelings, but into the space that is full of power and possibility and which encompasses the heart *and* the mind? As it turns out, this is one area in which these parts agree. When all of the tools and abilities that we possess are laid out before us, neither the heart nor the mind can help but admire one another. We begin to see not what we want or need or don't have, but what we are currently capable of – today. Once we begin to change our line of questioning, our emotions and reason become suddenly empowered, each in their own way. As coaches, we ask powerful questions; clients respond, and in return begin to ask the powerful questions for themselves. This is the value of coaching. When the heart and mind are each questioned and then listened to, we are able to see what it is we truly desire, and we know how to get it.

Cindy

I recently worked with a client who was struggling intensely with these very issues. Cindy wanted to work with a coach as a means of revamping her current life, which felt extremely unbalanced. Cindy's job at a successful real estate company was extremely draining, both mentally and physically. As we moved together through the coaching process, Cindy revealed that in college, she had been a highly creative person, painting vast, colorful murals and abstract canvases, sometimes working throughout the night. She told me that painting made her feel free, alive, and sure-footed. Cindy became a realtor because she enjoyed the light and energy of houses and spaces, and she wanted to surround herself with these elements. At first, she really enjoyed this work. As time wore on, the stress of her 60-hour work week began to wear her down. She felt tired and drained, and depressed about how little time she had for her own dreams and goals. She found it extremely difficult to nurture her creative self. She woke up, went to the office, came home late, ate alone, went to bed and then woke up and did it all over again the next day, for six days a week. She spent so much time focused on work, she simply didn't have enough energy left over for herself. Specifically, she never had enough time to feed her creative self.

When I asked Cindy what her ideal creative life would look like, she paused. "You know", she said, "it wouldn't even be that much. I just need to know that I am doing it, being creative."

"What will that give you, knowing that you are being creative?" I asked.

"It will give me Myself", she said. "And *balance*."

For Cindy, the feeling of nurturing her own creative spirit was almost more important than the creation of art itself. Painting made her feel free, in control and — most importantly — aligned with her true self. It was an important fixture of her life for many years, before her demanding career began to take over.

When I asked Cindy what her work limits were, she said quickly that she would never quit her job. She was only five years away from retirement, she reasoned, and she would never give up the security and financial stability that her job afforded her. In this sense, Cindy's mind / heart balance was disproportionate. Her intrinsic, deeply personal relationship with herself was being sacrificed to another, perhaps equally important, need for her own continuing financial stability. The task was how to bring these two needs together: the desire to express her creative voice and her need for financial security. Characteristically, the mind and heart, once pitted against each other in such a way, begin to bicker. Usually one has a considerably louder voice than the other (in Cindy's case, her intellectual self controlled her actions and choices: the need for security took precedence over that of creativity). It's no surprise that we struggle to make changes in our lives when our main decision-making centers are so divided. After detailed exploration into her own wants and desires, Cindy arrived at this mind-bending, all-powerful question: how to bridge this divide between her reasoning and her emotions?

As international coach and motivational speaker Brian Tracy says: "You are a living magnet; you attract into your life people, situations and circumstances that are in harmony with your dominant thoughts. Whatever you dwell on in your conscious grows into your experience" (Tracy,16). The way that we think about and process the things in our lives directly affects the outcome of our actions and choices. Our reality is based on what we think and feel, not on the things that happen to us.

When we ask powerful questions, we begin to challenge that way of thinking. "What is this getting me? What is this costing me? Who would I be if this stress were lifted? What do I value about this situation / choice / experience?" Powerful questions serve as a sort of magnifying glass, under which we can examine the origin of our thoughts and feelings. When we begin to understand the thought's value or limitation, we give ourselves the power to invest in or dismiss that way of thinking. In doing so, we can begin to change not only our thoughts, but also our lives.

For Cindy, the answer to her all-important question was found only once she was able to listen actively to both her heart and mind, and the thoughts they were generating. She quickly discovered that she wanted to keep her job, but she needed to make some changes first. After reflecting on her emotional life - in other words, her heart energy - Cindy discovered that she needed to give her creativity a stronger voice in order to feed her continued professional success. Within one session, Cindy had prioritized and set in place a new desired outcome, based on an intense questioning of her current thoughts and feelings.

After a number of sessions together, the question of available support came up. But it wasn't me who asked the question – it was Cindy. Before I had the chance to speak, she said "So I guess I should ask myself what resources I have?"

She had graduated from being a client, answering the questions I tossed her, to operating from a more masterful, self-aware position, asking herself the powerful questions automatically, and without pause.

By identifying and noticing her resources (friends and family, co-workers and a local art center, not to mention her own ingenuity and determination), Cindy was able to focus her energy on these positive factors in her life. She was able to direct her attention and thoughts to what was *already there* - though hidden from view - rather then on what was lacking. When she began to notice the areas in which she felt truly fulfilled and supported, Cindy's heart and mind began to achieve balance. And now she had something new: the ability to challenge herself with powerful questions. It was time for Cindy to make some big changes in her life. She tentatively pitched the idea of cutting down some of her hours to her boss who, to her surprise, had noticed Cindy's recent lack of energy. He fully supported the idea and she managed to cut a few of her work hours and rearrange her schedule, making enough time for herself and for her art.

Sarah and Todd

During a coffee date with a friend, Sarah, who has been having some marital problems with her husband Todd. She told me that lately their relationship had begun to feel one-sided. She claimed that she was the only one who 'took action' when things needed to get done. From paying bills to choosing where to go on vacation, Sarah felt like she was the only functioning partner in their relationship. When I asked what things Todd *did* do to contribute, she looked embarrassed. "Well," she said "He tries to help, but he never does anything right – so I just end up doing it myself."

By our second cup of coffee, the truth came out. "We just don't really talk to each other much anymore," she confessed. "I feel like we want different things now. But I know we wanted the same things in the beginning – somehow we just drifted away from that". Sarah said that since their recent drop in communication, she has been feeling the need to take charge, simply because she felt like the only participant in the relationship. After responding to the positively framed question: "What does Todd do to contribute?", the change in Sarah's emotional state, both physically (evidenced by her posture and expression) and emotionally, was palpable. She had visibly gone from a purely mind-centric way of examining her problems to a more emotional, heart-based one. The shift in balance was clear to both of us.

Lack of communication, trust and balance are common enough complaints in a long-term romantic partnership. It's not easy connecting daily about a myriad of interwoven details and life decisions, trying to maintain harmony and peace while tackling life's challenges and stresses as they crop up. The challenge is how to keep all working parts of the relationship strengthened and functioning, both from a place of heart and a place of mind.

When asked, "What *is* working in the relationship?" Sarah told me about some of their strengths as a couple: the ability to laugh and make jokes, a shared love of cooking, their passion for planning trips and traveling. Again, when Sarah mused over the parts of their relationship that *were* working, her perception completely changed. For her, focusing on the hidden overlying strengths in a relationship was one way to shift the dialogue from a negative standpoint to a more positive one. Being aware of a couple's individual and shared strengths - both emotional and mental - can help them to find a more peaceful, relaxed place from which to conduct their relationship. Think of a Venn Diagram, where logical relationships between certain "sets" are illustrated to display like features. Noticing their interlocking abilities and traits, a couple can learn to operate from a position of unity and strength – from the center of the Venn Diagram, rather then opposite sides. A couple's common interests and abilities show the best parts of their relationship - and the reasons why they fell in love in the first place.

Venn Diagram

Looking at the relationship in this way can also help each person in the couple to recalibrate, individually finding their way back to a more balanced state. In Sarah's case, when she began to ask herself questions about their common interests and strengths, she quickly saw the areas in which she was dominating the relationship. Sarah realized that she needed to give Todd the chance to make choices and participate as an equal partner in their marriage. Just as our rational thoughts sometimes have to give way to our emotions, so Sarah realized that she needed to hand some power and accountability over to Todd.

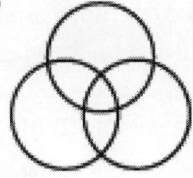

The mind / heart relationship can also function like a couple. When the heart and mind lose the ability to really connect, making decisions together can feel next to impossible. And like any couple, they need to continually seek new ways of communicating. Even the process of initiating a dialog between the two disparate parts can serve to balance them. Ask yourself what conflicting needs and wants you might have. For example, in Cindy's case, these were centered around the need for financial security and the desire for individual creativity, two seemingly different things. For her, addressing both and then examining ways to make each heard and respected allowed the unbalanced parts to co-exist. Do you have needs and wants that seem to clash in this way? Identify what they are, and then ask yourself, what do they represent about your values and beliefs? What are the fundamental reasons for *having these* needs and wants in the first place? How might they be serving / limiting you? Are your mind and heart in equal balance?

Seek out the strengths that your mind and heart possess in regard to a certain life area. Write them down. For example:

Mind: My mind helps me keep myself in check when spending money. I know that I have a budget and I remind myself of this so I won't overspend. I keep track of the numbers, noticing what I spend and what I save. I can't afford this!

Heart: My heart tells me that its okay to splurge once in a while, that it makes me feel good to give myself what I want. If I buy this _____, it will give me a lot of pleasure.

Notice any recurring strengths in the different areas. What are they giving you? What message might your mind / heart be trying to send? For example, a particular recurring strength might be: "my mind tells me intellectually whether I'm making the right decision, and my heart tells me intuitively." In this case, both the cerebral and emotion-based centers are key factors in making a decision: each serves a purpose in the experience. Like holding down parallel sides of a see saw, both carry an equal weight. Each are necessary ingredients for making well-balanced, thoughtful decisions. Listening to and legitimizing both the heart and mind will allow them each to feel heard and validated, and they will in turn fall into a loving relationship, rather than allowing one to take precedence over the other.

Take Five

It seems like a simple, obvious solution to a stressful or discordant situation: taking a moment to just breathe and get centered. Stopping and getting just a bit retrospective has always helped me to pull my heart and mind back together in moments of unease or strain, and allows me to get in touch with my deeper, intuitive feelings rather than those based on outside expectations or pressure.

This method of handling stress is great on two levels: first, it is adaptable to fit any situation. In other words, you can take five minutes, one hour, or ten seconds, and you can do this virtually anywhere. Second, once you begin to introduce this habit it will become increasingly automatic; you will find yourself stopping and re-centering without even knowing you are doing it.

To use this tool, you must first recognize moments of stress for what they are – stressful! Begin by simply paying attention when you begin to feel overwhelmed, frustrated or pressured. (Many of us go through the day feeling constantly triggered yet we don't notice when it's happening.) Write down any patterns around these stressful situation: do they happen at the same time of the day, with the same people, at the same places? Then, when a stressful situation occurs, take a moment to close your eyes and notice your breathing. Focus all of your energy on the inside of yourself, drawing your attention away from the external and to the internal. The first few times using this tool, you may have to take yourself out of the situation and go to a private place, such as the restroom or to an empty room. Then, simply ask yourself this question:

How would it feel to let this stressful feeling go?

Letting go of a stressful thought or feeling, whether it comes from the heart or the head, can set you free. As the Peace Pilgrim said, "if you realized how powerful our thoughts are, you would never think a negative thought." This can be most helpful for those of us who are highly reactive to stress and need a quick and surefire way to stop and re-center ourselves. Taking a moment to stop and breathe, then simply asking this question gives enormous added perspective and peace. When we use our ability to put the heart and mind in charge, rather than giving power to an external event or person, we take control. By bringing the heart and head together in a meaningful and positive way, you are ultimately creating a much stronger intuitive relationship with yourself. Developing this dialog between the two parts strengthens their relationship, balancing both sides and helping the mind and heart to communicate effectively and positively.

Paris

I can recall many times in my life where my mind / heart connection felt out of balance. Perhaps one of the most powerful memories I have of this was when I met my husband, Yann, who is French. We had been friends and pen pals in our adolescence, but we hadn't seen one another in nearly eight years. In 2009 I left South Korea, where I had been living and working for two years, and went to Paris for a week's vacation. I decided to give him a call. We agreed to meet in the 10th arrondissement, at a tiny restaurant with a cobblestone courtyard and a beautiful outdoor terrace. We spent hours there, well into the night, talking and catching up on all that we had missed over the past eight years. I could feel my heart already starting to ache in my chest, and I felt that this was the man I was supposed to spend my life with.

I was scheduled to return to the States the following day, and Yann was leaving for Spain. He took me to the station, and I forced myself to get on board. When the train pulled away from the platform, I could feel my heart beginning to hurt again. But how could I feel so connected to someone I barely knew?

I returned home and brooded. Even though we knew each other from childhood, essentially we were strangers. Suddenly, my practical, thought-based responses started to kick in and do battle with my heart. I wanted to go back to France – and could go back in fact, as it had been cheaper to purchase a round trip ticket even though I had only needed a one-way. The return date for the ticket was for the next week. If I went, how would I tell my friends and family that I was planning to leave, right after I had just gotten home for the first time in two years? It was completely insane on all levels: put everything on the line, give up a *great* job I had just landed in Seattle, and move to France for a man I just spent approximately 24 hours with. Great. For a chiefly rational thinker like me, this was an enormously complicated decision. And yet here I was. I desperately wanted to go and be with him, but my head told me shut up and be practical.

A week later, I packed my bags, said goodbye (again), and boarded a plane for France. I can't tell you much about the pushing and pulling that went on in my brain during that week at home, but I do remember this: one night, mulling over what to do, a question came to me:

"What do you have to lose?"

And I suddenly realized, no matter what happened, I would never regret going to France – even if the relationship didn't work out. I thought about my friends and family who loved me, and would still love me, regardless of where I lived. I thought about the times in my life where I have shown strength and courage, and knew that I had the courage to do this too. And suddenly, my mind conceded to what my heart was saying and went quiet. All of the "buts" and "what if's" were silenced. With one question, I had found the key to balancing my heart and mind: trust. Both emotionally and intellectually, I knew I could trust I was doing the right thing for myself. I also knew I could get hurt, suffer financially, and cause pain. However, when I looked into the deepest part of myself, I saw I had a safety net all around me, and falling into it actually *was* an option.

And so I fell. As it turned out, I didn't need the net. But just knowing it was there gave me confidence to move forward into unknown territory. Since I had listened to my rational mind and acknowledged its wants and needs, I was able to move forward with a feeling of balance and inner peace, no matter what happened. I saw that both my heart and mind had given me a great amount of information about my needs and desires, and who I was as a person. After taking it all in, I was able to make an informed decision.

When the dialog between the heart and mind becomes stuck, unbalanced, or is simply nonexistent, the solution can be found in a simple question. Taking a moment to stop, breathe, and ask ourselves "what do I have" helps shift our perspective away from this negative, fear-based line of thinking. If we take the time to listen to the heart *and* mind and consider what they might be trying to tell us, we will see the value in what they each have to say. Allowing ourselves to move into this positive, coach-like manner of questioning our thoughts and feelings will allow both the heart and mind to feel important and championed, bringing us closer to balance and, ultimately, peace.

Questions for Reflection:

- Where do your heart and mind connect?

- Where do they collide the most?

- What might be possible if they found a way to work together?

Sources

Tracy, Brian. The 100 Absolutely Unbreakable Laws of Business Success. San Francisco: Berrett-Koehler Publishers, Inc. 2002

Peace Pilgrim. www.peacepilgrim.org

About Veronica Bishop

Veronica Bishop, CPC is an educator, writer and certified professional life coach with a focus on health and fitness. After teaching English as a second language in both South Korea and France, she and her husband moved from Paris to Portland, where she has pursued her true dream of working as a coach.

She is certified as a Whole Person Coach through the Baraka Institute and now runs her own coaching business, Bishop Coaching. She believes that coaching, similar to teaching, is powerful because it allows the client be wholly in control of the direction and design that they want to use to create the next steps in their lives. Working as a health coach has allowed her to make hugely positive and transformational changes in her own life, and she enjoys working individually with clients to facilitate and encourage their own personal life transformations.

In her spare time, she loves reading, hiking and running, hunting secondhand shops for treasures and drinking red wine outdoors with her husband.

www.veronica.tsfl.com

Extraordinary
Understandings
FOR AN ORDINARY LIFE

by Suzanne Shafer

We cannot know what will change us. We can only listen for the
moment when something in us wants our permission to breathe.
Thankfully I was paying attention in the summer of 1983, when
I spent two weeks wrestling with a question that changed my life:
"Should I buy the beautiful blue couch?"

My apartment was filled with brown—a color with which I had
surrounded myself for a decade, though I didn't actually like it. It was
practical and safe. It went with all the carpets in all the apartments
into which I was perpetually moving. I was thirty-three and everything
was about "fitting in." Like a chameleon, I turned whatever color was
necessary to make myself acceptable to others. I knew that doing this
didn't make me happy, but I couldn't question the off-the-rack life into
which I was trying to squeeze.

It was easy to know who others thought I should be, and I
excelled at playing by their rules. I was earning a graduate degree in a
profession prescribed by my father, though I knew I would never love
it. I attended the church of my childhood, though I couldn't embrace
its dogma. And, already twice married and divorced, I still dreamed of
that man who would provide me the perfect, ready-made life and love

me forever, just as I was. I had not yet recognized my own invisibility, and thus couldn't question how difficult it might be for anyone to see and love the "me" who was such a closely kept secret.

It is strange to meet oneself for the first time in a discount furniture warehouse. But there was the couch—the perfect color, the perfect shape, the perfect price. With love-at-first-sight clarity I *knew* that my brown-saturated heart cherished rich blue. I knew this, but stood frozen in a second question: "What if I meet *him* and he hates my blue couch?"

I had been catapulted into a struggle with what scared me most— the possibility that, if seen, my true color would not be loved. My days and dreams rang with the question "How can I risk it?" I could think of little else. Then one morning, without fanfare, I awoke knowing that the anxious "What if..." that so often stopped me would not rule this time. "If *he* cannot love me because he prefers brown, so be it. I have chosen the blue couch." It was a notable moment, but not one of transformational insight. Only in retrospect do I recognize it as the day on which the frightened chameleon began its l-o-n-g, s-l-o-w death march.

Many years have passed since I invited the blue couch into my life. Most friends to whom I tell this story today look at me in disbelief. They see an independent, accomplished woman. They know the vibrant, eclectic energy of my home—a space that expresses the self that drew its first full breath when I defied the mythical *him*. Only occasionally does the chameleon, not yet fully expired, slither into view.

The blue couch had beckoned me toward a transformational path and I began my journey. But I would travel for nearly thirty years thinking that I had taken a wrong turn. Somehow I had failed, for my life was supposed to have been extraordinary.

As a toddler I survived spinal meningitis in an era when few children did. Many times I had heard my parents' story of a night spent in prayer for my life. It always ended with the solemn injunction, "God saved you for something special." It was a heady message with which to grow up, and by my late twenties it had become a burden.

I believed that "special" meant living a uniquely exciting life that captured hearts and made me famous. It meant others wanting to know what *I* thought and wanting to live *my* life which, of course, would inspire a book and become a movie. It didn't mean holding jobs that bored me, marrying men who battered me, or feeling hopelessly locked into self-sabotaging patterns. Above all, it did not mean having the constant sense that I was waiting for my *real* life to begin.

I envied everyone who appeared to know what their lives were about, for nothing I did felt meaningful. I knew other people saw me as a woman with diverse interests and valuable skills, but I considered my life mundane. I was an onlooker, just filling time while I waited for my glowing future. I looked in many places for the passionate experiences I saw happening in the lives of people I admired, but my life was composed of ordinary days, one after another. With each one that passed it seemed more apparent that I would never have that special life for which I had been saved.

Waiting for my extraordinary life had become a disabling preoccupation, an obstacle to my peace of mind. This is obvious to me now, but only recently have I recognized it.

Early one morning in March of 2011, I awoke from a fitful sleep in the mood for a really big gripe. I brewed a pot of strong coffee then sat down at my dining room table with my journal, prepared to savor the experience. Picking up my favorite pen, I began with these words, "Sometimes, being a strong, single, senior woman just sucks. I don't mean to complain. This is simply an observation."

Actually, I *did* mean to complain. I had just been discharged from the hospital, after an emergency surgery to remove my gallbladder. Four days earlier, I had awakened at three a.m., in excruciating pain. Instead of calling for help right away, I had waited six hours before summoning an ambulance. "What if it is just gas?" blithered the old chameleon. "That would be so humiliating!"

Now, alone and uncomfortable with the bandages and tubes, I felt vulnerable. I longed for someone's company but was immobilized by a prospect much more threatening to my self-image than the possibility of dialing 911 for flatulence. "I am afraid that if I ask for what I really want right now—to have someone here just to witness my misery and care about me in this wretched moment—I will discover that I can't have it. I will learn that no one cares enough to be here with me, and that I am stuck with being the strong woman I tell myself others expect me to be."

With that confession, I closed my journal. I knew what to expect. I had just acknowledged something that made me deeply uncomfortable, and in my experience, facing one difficult truth usually invites the arrival of another. This time, the truth awaiting my consideration was preceded by a week of being confronted with a question I was desperate to avoid. "Who am I, *really*, and what do I *really* want?"

I could think of nothing so mortifying as the possibility that I still might not have an answer to this deeply familiar query. A year earlier, after a long period of indecision, I had trained to become a life coach. Pouring myself into my new pursuit, I had told everyone I *finally* knew what my life was about. My friends had applauded my decision, pulled me through moments of self-doubt, and celebrated each success as I began to build a practice. How could I admit that I still felt the fear and uncertainty I had always believed would dissipate when my "real life" finally began?

Did my lack of courage and clarity mean I had again chosen poorly? Would being a life coach become as irrelevant to me as the several careers I had already left behind? Would I someday abandon this path as I had so many other possibilities that had seemed promising?

I have learned that when I am ready to hear deep truths, my heart will provide them. Sitting down with my journal the following Saturday morning, I resolved to let my heart speak, no matter how disturbing I might find its messages. When I laid down my pen hours later, I felt a deep and confident peace. I had learned who I am and what I have to offer.

As wonderful as that may sound, my heart wanted to give me something even more important. It announced its next gift by prompting my curiosity. "When did I begin keeping this journal?" Reopening it, I read an entry dated a decade earlier—an entry in which the doubts of the past week, and many of the insights I had just written, were represented.

The realization of how long I had been repeating myself had only begun to register when the words of my personal mission statement, written several years before the ten-year-old journal entry, formed in my mind as if on the page before me. Startled by the clarity of what suddenly confronted me, I began to weep.

The evidence was inescapable. When it chose the blue couch, my heart had already known where my joy resided, and ever since, had guided my journey toward it. Vision, insight and ability had become mine as I traveled. Yet I had progressed slowly because the chameleon, always timid, retreated to the safe and familiar whenever success in a new endeavor was beyond guarantee. With this revelation I understood that, in spite of what was now so clear, I might easily spend the *next* ten years repeating this pattern.

My heart posed the question that most needed an answer: "If not now, when?" At the age of 33, I had made a decision that changed my life. On a drizzly Saturday in the spring of my 61st year, I made yet another. I stopped waiting for an extraordinary future and embraced my ordinary life. I decided to honor and share the lessons it has provided me, for they are what I have to offer *now*. An astonishing parade of events has since followed, as the life that was only awaiting my consent has begun to unfold.

On that morning when I was ready to listen, my heart invited me to humility; it spoke the wisdom of many authors whose work I'd read while searching for the secret that would make my life extraordinary. Long an antidote to my sense of failure, the books in my personal library are rich with ideas that fascinate me. But as I wrote that morning, a small handful of these ideas emerged from that wealth as if in a spotlight.

These were familiar ideas I had encountered many times during my journey, my understanding of them deepening with each reappearance. Yet, as I expressed them that morning, each concept felt new. And as I wrote, I recognized *them* as the "extraordinary" in my life. I saw how they had moved me steadily forward, shaping my journey and enhancing my capacity for growth.

While these Extraordinary Understandings have become my foundation for transformation, I cannot know whether they will resonate with you, for each of us is responsible to decide what constitutes our truth. Nonetheless, I offer them in the hope that you will find at least a few that support and enlarge your vision of what is possible. Though I consider their order inconsequential, I introduce these ideas in the chronology of my first encounter with them. For some, I share the context of the encounter because it remains an event from which I continue to learn, and a story that I now share with those I teach. I invite you to consider whether these ideas, so powerful in my own life, might also benefit yours, and I offer some questions to deepen your reflection.

Ten Extraordinary Understandings

1. Step up to fear; it is an unavoidable part of the human condition.

I was raised in a home ruled by fear, and it has dictated many of my life choices. Even now, fear rarely leaves my side. I no longer ask it to. I have learned that it is essential; my fear of staying stuck in my fears is what ultimately compels me to take new steps in the direction of my dreams. It is from the act of moving forward in the face of anxiety that I gain the deepest understanding of who I am, who I might become, and what it means to be human.

We cannot transform until we agree to move directly into our fears. This is how we learn that we can survive them. It is how we discover we are bigger than what frightens us. Step into your fears; you *will* survive them, but you cannot know this until you do!

> *For Contemplation — What is the fear you most wish to be without? What could you do to step into it?*

2. No matter what they are, you are not alone in your imperfections.

In my late thirties, I fell in love with a man who told me he was codependent. Melody Beattie had just published *Codependent No More* and I rushed out to buy it, knowing I could fix him and live happily ever after. I soon realized the joke was on me, and I remember the catharsis of laughter and tears as I recognized myself in every page. The "me" I tried so hard to hide—a woman whose vulnerable façade perpetually threatened to crumble— had been "out-ed" and it was marvelous! Oh how hard I worked to keep others from knowing what was beneath the competent exterior I managed to don each morning! How terrified I was of the rejection I was certain would follow if others glimpsed the disaster I believed myself to be. And oh, how liberating it was to realize that, messy as I might be, I was only one among legions!

That evening, when I laid down Melody's book, I had joined the human race.

If you are still in hiding, I invite you to do the same. Healing lies in letting go of the dubious prestige that accompanies the illusion of being exceptionally flawed. I have been learning this, and relearning it, every day since.

> *For Contemplation – Which of your flaws makes you "exceptional" and who would you be if you no longer considered it significant?*

3. Your life can be no larger than your vision of who you are meant to be.

Shortly after I began the second of my four careers, my workgroup was scheduled for five days of training based on Stephen Covey's book, *The 7 Habits of Highly Effective People*. On our first day in the classroom, the instructor invited us into a powerful experience by asking us to transport ourselves—figuratively, of course—to our own funerals. He suggested that we sit among the mourners and listen to what they were saying about us.

This was a seminal moment, for when I arrived at my imagined wake, there was no one there! Thankfully, the wisdom of this exercise was in the instruction to hear what I *wanted* others to say about me, so I swallowed hard and spoke my own eulogies. As I did, I suddenly understood why the room was empty. *I could not think of a single person who would have any reason to say what I wanted to hear! Not one!* My life was about me in every respect. I would have protested any description of myself as "self-absorbed", but it's difficult to argue with an unattended funeral. There was a priceless gift in the well-placed blow delivered to my ego that day. My heart knew a truth that my life did not evidence, and with my shell broken open, it told its secret: I dreamed of benefitting others in ways that enabled them to manifest their potential.

The exercise was a prelude for the real work that day—composing a personal mission statement. I took the assignment seriously, and what I wrote then still expresses who I wish to be in this world. What astonishes me now is that this mission statement—written when the word "coach" meant nothing more to me than a guy on the sidelines of a Monday night football game—perfectly reflects what I now strive to create in every coaching relationship, and in my own life. That day, I wrote:

For each Tomorrow, I will leave a legacy of having—with Courage, Compassion, and Creativity—helped others to open deeply to the limitless possibilities within themselves, and inspired them to their own greatness. *In each Today,* I will practice my Personal Accountability for composing a life that gives voice and touch to my truths.

I knew I was not prepared to deliver on this mission. The challenge would require a deep commitment to grow into a life I could not yet visualize. This is the nature of a vision: if it does not push you beyond what you imagine are the limits of your potential, it is not as big as you can be.

Allow yourself to dream well beyond who you think you are today. Nothing less will catalyze action. Only the really big dreams can motivate you to move through the inevitable fear.

For Contemplation – What do you most long to hear others say of you, and who might you need to become in order to say that of yourself?

4. We choose our stories, and through them we create our lives.
In my mid-forties, I met the first of three special teachers who would each enrich my life with an Understanding. A colleague dubbed the first one "The Velvet-Toothed Piranha" and explained the odd moniker by saying, "He goes straight for the jugular and lets some very toxic blood, without tearing your flesh." It was a perfect description of my first fifteen minutes in this teacher's presence. Swiftly, yet without injury, Piranha Number One shredded my belief that my miseries were created by my dysfunctional family, my ex-husbands, and the bosses who failed to appreciate me. I shaped my own experience, he said, with *my* thoughts about myself and others. This was a novel idea to one who had, over

many years, crafted a volume of exquisite stories confirming her victimhood. It got my attention.

Many teachers now express the idea that was then so new to me. In most moments of most days, we tell ourselves stories and believe them to be true. It is what humans do; it is how we create meaning and that's not likely to change. Our stories are habitual and our storylines often repetitious. We accept them without question, and thus they create our lives. When our stories are happy, so are we. When they are disempowering or disparaging, we suffer and we create suffering around us.

See the evidence in your own experience. When you tell yourself that you absolutely cannot do a thing, do you rush toward the next opportunity to discover that you can? When you tell yourself a story of joy, do you not pursue whatever your storyline has named as its source?

Most of us tell ourselves stories that get in our way. If you have recognized this tendency in your own storytelling and are ready to renounce it, there is very good news: if a tale isn't working for you, as its author, you can change it. Indeed, the only thing truly within your control is your choice of story. Accepting this provides transformative leverage. Failing to do so results in an untested narrative that creates the same feelings, actions, and results in perpetuity.

It takes courage to discard a familiar story, especially a self-sabotaging one. It requires commitment to try on a new story in the service of your personal vision. But while neither is easy, these choices come with a guarantee. They *will* change your life.

> *For Contemplation – What do you most often say about yourself and how has this scripted your life?*

5. Contribution is not optional. Your happiness depends on it.

I knew Piranha Number Two for half an hour. While attending an intense, personal growth workshop, I was allowed a private consultation with one of the gifted teachers. I chose to spend 25 of my 30 minutes complaining about how my parents had failed me.

The Piranha listened until I finished, then, her hand on my shoulder and face close to mine, remarked, "It is very sad that you did not feel loved when you were young. Every child deserves to know that they are special. The fact that you did not learn this will make it more difficult, but...(there was a loaded pause) it is time for you to begin giving to the world what you believe you did not receive. You will not thrive until you do." With that, the consultation ended.

I left that room in silence and began an uphill climb toward the discovery that abundance becomes most apparent when I set out to give what I perceive is in short supply. With each attempt to do this, I find within me the perfect measure of whatever is needed.

There is no doubt that the course and terrain of your path will be influenced by your history. You may feel so damaged or emptied by what you have experienced that you can see no way to give. I know that feeling well. I also know that ultimately, to reach a destination worthy of effort, we must each allow our history to take a back seat to the question, "Are you contributing what you would most like to receive?"

For Contemplation – What was there not enough of for you? How might you offer that into the world?

6. Impermanence is a given. Cherish your vision, but hold loosely your ideas of how it must unfold.

As I was leaving my office one evening after a very long day of work, the personnel manager asked, "Suzanne, do you have a minute?" Fifteen minutes later, I knew that the world I had created for myself was gone. I would be unemployed within the week. Without a job, I would soon lose my home, for I was deeply in debt and had nothing set aside.

There was no last-minute rescue. I *did* lose the life into which I had poured so many of my resources. I lost the future I had been certain I was creating. When I began to rebuild six months later, it was in a place and under circumstances I never would have recommended had Life consulted me. Yet, from that "disaster" has come much of what I now value most.

A collision with impermanence can feel crazy-making. Though it is obvious that transformation requires us to let go of what holds us back, we are wary of change and we try to avoid being surprised by it. We work hard to ensure that our lives unfold "according to plan," with as little upset as possible. But the wheels we set in motion to ensure our prosperity or to spare us from pain cannot do so.

The creativity essential to transformation does not arise from surety and stasis. Life is fluid. It encompasses joy and heartbreak, progress and retreat, certainty and fear. Transformation lies in transcending what we once believed to be indisputable. What we know in any moment, what we are able to believe in *this* moment, is but a speck of the infinitude available to us.

To grasp anything tightly in order to protect yourself from the unnerving vastness of uncertainty, is to lock down your heart, making it unavailable to life in its fullness. Flow is inevitable; let it happen and let yourself happen with it.

For Contemplation – What one thing would you be willing to hold onto less tightly, even for one day?

7. Greet your flaws with compassion. They are your perfect teachers.

When I become perfect… I will cease to learn. Thankfully, I'm in no danger of perfection. Nor are you. Our flaws stick around until we learn the perfect lessons they offer, and when we have done so, fresh imperfections replace them. This is something you can count on; it is a condition of being human, and whatever you have to contribute will flow from recognizing and accepting this.

The truth is, you cannot be more kind-hearted toward the imperfections of others than you are toward your own. Self-compassion is essential to transformation. Compassion for others is its fruit.

For Contemplation — Which of your flaws has taught you the most valuable lessons? How might you show more compassion toward yourself and others when this flaw manifests?

8. Transformation requires that action be balanced with stillness.

When Susan Jeffers published *Feel the Fear and Do It Anyway*, I adopted its title as my motto and began to overcome the paralysis that was often my response to fear. This was right and timely, but it was not sufficient. I did not yet understand that while fear could freeze me, it could also compel me to take actions that served only to help me avoid the discomfort of uncertainty.

When I was troubled, I felt driven to "work things out." For years I fled to action to divert my attention from inner despair that needed to be acknowledged and metabolized. I didn't perceive this as problematic, for I usually chose action that resulted in new skills and accomplishments. Or so it seemed until I met Piranha Number Three, who was my teacher for ten years. Repeatedly he pointed out how habitually, and often enthusiastically, I expressed my unresolved misery by acting in ways that disempowered or harmed me.

Because I truly wanted to grow and trusted his wisdom, I frequently asked my teacher for his opinion about things I felt compelled to do. Not once did he give it. Instead, he always offered me a single, frustrating pearl: "Sit with it."

The Chinese call this sitting *wu wei*, or "choosing expectant waiting." Others call it patience or faith. Whatever you call it, when you begin to practice stillness you will discover it can be far more difficult than action. It requires relinquishing the need to control, for this is essential to creating the space in which your understanding of what is truly necessary will grow.

How can we know when stillness is requisite? My heart knows. It can discern when a particular action will only enable me to avoid an openness essential to my unfolding. If I create the opportunity, it will tell me. I now trust this as deeply as I once trusted my teacher. Your heart knows, too. So sit with it. Just sit with it.

For Contemplation – What question in your life might it benefit you to "sit with" right now?

9. We have only this moment.

"What Is" may not be what I asked for, nor what I think it should be, but no argument I make will change it. Might things have played out differently had *I* been different? Perhaps. But I'm not and they didn't. Might I be happier if he, she, or it were different? They aren't, nor can I make them be, so I will never know.

The present moment has evolved from the reality of the moments before it. We cannot change either. "Now" is a perfect place from which to begin or continue transformation. It holds both our histories and exactly what we need to move toward who we will become.

I am enough for this moment. I have always been. And so have you.

For Contemplation – Who would you be without your favorite argument against the Now of your life?

10. We are connected.

Describe this connection to yourself in any way that empowers you and fills you with joy, and you will be right. We can only describe—inadequately—our own experience of connection, for it precedes and transcends every word ever uttered about it. But though words fail to express it, we can *know* ourselves to be connected. And when we do, our capacity for becoming who we are meant to be is enlarged. The essence of connection is an ongoing act of creative transformation. So make a practice of doing whatever allows you to experience it: take a moment to observe your breath coming and going without your volition, involving you intimately with everything it touches; enter a holy space, indoors or out, in which your mind rests and your heart swells; notice the joy inherent in an experience of the beautiful, and savor the awe accompanying any small moment of understanding what it means to be connected.

For Contemplation – When are you most likely to experience an energy that expands your spirit and opens your heart? How often are you willing to allow yourself that connection?

~~~~~~~~~~~~~~~~~~

For many years I mourned the extraordinary life that had not materialized as I envisioned. I no longer do so. I understand now that I will always be a traveler and that the journey itself provides all that I have to contribute to the lives of others. Today I know that what I have to offer is good enough, and that from the stream of my ordinary life flow truth, wisdom and joy. What is more, the very ordinariness and length of my journey, with its deficit of front-page happenings, makes it the perfect experience from which to speak to the many others who, like me, have said, "It is too late." For I know today that I am exactly where I need to be! I believe you are, too.

About Suzanne Shafer

Suzanne Shafer, MN, CPC

Ask Suzanne about herself and she's likely to respond, "I'm old." Then she'll grin and tell you that "old" is wonderful. She saw 60 come and go before she knew who she wanted to be when she grew up, and she believes every year was essential to what she now contributes as a teacher, writer, and coach. Suzanne loves working with people in transition. Whether you are moving to a place you've never seen, going back to school, falling in or out of love, dieting, changing careers, or wondering who you *really* are, she's been there and knows how unnerving it can be. "I've done much of my life the hard way," she'll say. She thinks this is a good thing because she knows, firsthand, that difficult experiences are great opportunities to grow. Suzanne's professional experience includes over 40 years in a wide variety of healthcare roles, including nurse, therapist, administrator, researcher, educator, change facilitator, and consultant. She believes life is about learning—which she does as she works with her clients, plays in the outdoors, volunteers in her community, and finds joy in dancing, reading, writing, gardening, and traveling.

www.TheIntentionalExcellenceCoach.com

the value of Recollection

by Yvonne Anello

In my family, life is described as a journey on a road full of twists and turns. I was taught that to fully experience life's road, it is important to take in the sights, sounds, cities and towns along the way. Each milestone evokes strong memories, and depending on our responses to the changes presented along the way, we may be seductively lulled into a desire to settle and stop moving forward.

In this chapter I'd like to share an early segment of my journey and illustrate the process of recollecting and recapturing the inspiration of past successes and positive experiences to utilize as a template for decision-making. My technique includes four steps: 1) identifying today's challenge; 2) recalling a past milestone (experience) that resonates with the challenge; 3) objectively recording the specific thoughts, feelings and actions of the milestone; and 4) retelling the story of the milestone in a manner that reflects its meaning to you.

Identifying the challenge

At age 58 I've come to a few forks in the road, yet on arriving at this one I was surprised to find it a familiar place. In fact as I look around, the road hasn't changed much since I was 18 years old. This time however, I arrive as a time-worn warrior, an experienced matron who has taught children and adults to accomplish and achieve. I've enjoyed a rich marriage, happy family life, and fulfilling career. My challenge at this fork is to choose between two directions, either to continue working at a job that offers me security but that I no longer approach with joy; or to embark on a new career. I find myself asking the same question I did when I was 18 years old: "What do I do with my life now that I am all grown up?"

Recalling a point in time

I came of age in the seventies, a wondrous time when women demanded equality and the freedom to live their own lives and make their own decisions. In those days, the Afro was the hot hairstyle and hot pants decorated shapely legs accented with platform shoes. It was a time when the flavor of music changed and when a political crime exacerbated the culture shock of the sixties and forever changed the myth that was America.

My family is of Spanish descent, and like most immigrant families, each generation has become more and more American, leaving older traditions behind. We started breaking tradition early. In the tumultuous fifties and sixties, my parents learned to move with the times and prepare their children for their individual journeys. Understanding that we needed to compete and succeed in white America, they moved us away from the extended family in the city and placed us smack in the middle of a predominately white suburb in Colorado. When later we moved to Oregon, it was such a drastic change for the extended family they could only assume my father moved us to hide an imagined shame.

My own road wound its way within that time. I watched white American culture on TV and in the movies, and saw it in our neighborhood. My parents challenged me as an outsider, to think about the life I wanted and to create that life without losing myself. They embraced their own culture, weaving the music, language and lifestyle of our heritage into our daily life at home. As I came of age and prepared to leave, I savored the warm and lively ethnic tapestry we had created in our home.

I began my senior year in high school the fall of 1970, while the Vietnam War was center stage in the world. American culture, rebounding from the late sixties, was split between hawks and doves, white and black, the sober and the polluted. In this era, the good girls in our extended family would traditionally be kept close to their home and roots until they married. Very few defied their parents. They'd receive a moderate education and learn how to care for a home, husband and children. If they had to, they would work in a job appropriate for an unmarried girl until they met their prospective husbands.

My parents certainly hoped I would meet someone I loved some day, but they didn't require anything of me except that I think first, be my best, and work hard to make my dreams come true. They were prepared to work their fingers to the bone to help me achieve what I wanted. Armed with this knowledge, I reached my first fork in the road while preparing to graduate from high school.

In October of my senior year, when our high school hosted a visit from the local military recruiting offices, I thought about my dad and his military service. Although the violence and horror of Vietnam was on TV each night, our family had a patriotic sentiment. My male cousins had been drafted to fight and my father had been a Marine during the Korean conflict. Well respected and dearly loved, my father was the family's champion and a hero in our extended family as well, willing and able to protect and serve.

At the recruitment meeting at school, the first service member to speak was a female Marine Corps sergeant, a meteorologist. While I entered the room clearly positioned at a fork in the road, a direction signal began flashing in bright colors when I heard her speak. After talking to the recruiter I found that I'd get my choice of duty station, which translated quickly to adventure. I'd have a home, clothes, and a regular paycheck! I'd be able to take care of myself. It added up to a solution to all my parents' worries. I came home and spoke to my parents about signing up.

They were taken aback, to say the least. Drugs, pre-marital sex and illegitimate children were not newly invented, but at this time in history they were being touted as a lifestyle. With race riots, protests for equal rights and the right to have abortions, how could they give their blessings or have confidence that I'd be prepared to be on my own in a world like this? To them, the sudden rise in the road must have seemed daunting, while all I anticipated was promise, adventure and freedom.

My poor parents! What did they do? They asked questions. Lots of them. Their eyes searched my face as I answered. They shared intimate looks with one another and then it was quiet. My mom said we would make an appointment to see the recruiter together. They gathered their "what ifs," packed them up and supported me.

My parents sat with me in the United States Marine Corps recruiting office and asked questions, seeking my input rather than telling me what to do or speaking for me. Mom was with me for my first vaginal exam, explaining it to me. When the actual exam left me feeling emotionally upset, she talked with me, as a woman and not as her little girl. Dad kept the chitchat about my upcoming departure to a minimum, but as we sat down together over dinner he began to tell us stories about his experiences as a Marine, giving me some insight into what I may be facing.

July 12, 1971, my departure day, remains one of the most important and heart-wrenching experiences of my life. Although I didn't understand the specific nature of my parents' feelings, I knew they were sad and concerned, despite their wishes for my happiness. But they treated me as an independent adult that day and not as their child. Mom looked me in the eye, said she loved me, and held me in the best embrace ever. I always knew she had faith in me as a person, that she knew deep inside that I'd be okay.

Dad, on the other hand, really surprised me. Because of my gender's second-rate importance in our culture, I didn't realize he thought I had prospects other than marrying one day and giving him grandchildren. Perhaps he expected no more than that. He used to tell us that we could be whatever we wanted to be, but somewhere along the line I believed he meant that truism for my brothers. He was the last to speak to me that morning. With tears welling in his eyes he put his hard hands on my shoulders and said, "I trust your judgment." I know he must have said more, but that's all I remember. I was so stunned that time stood still. I felt whole in a way that I can't describe. The hugs and kisses from my brothers and sisters were additional precious little gifts. My parents' final hugs and kisses enveloped me like armor as I turned and boarded the plane, Dad's words still echoing in my heart, I was officially launched and my life was my own.

Recording my thoughts about the past

It's now 2011, America is still trying to define itself, and I'm revisiting the old fork of my youth. How do I use my recollection above to motivate myself today?

Recently I entered a course of study to become a life coach. In class we worked through an exercise to create a timeline of achievement and used it to recollect these milestones with a coach. We practiced extracting the thoughts, feelings and actions that had merged together to create the achievements and discussed the details that made them memorable and meaningful. A streetlamp went on in my mind and the road was suddenly bathed in light. I understood that the value of recollection is to recapture the power and inspiration embodied in the memory.

In the recollection above, my thoughts, feelings and actions were fueled by the excitement of a new adventure and the profound confidence my parents had in me. Although I noticed doubt and fear presenting themselves at that time, I didn't dwell on them or give them power. In effect, I was not alone on my adventure, I was simply launched into a new segment of my life journey. To launch myself today it's important that I restate and reapply the gifts my family gave me at the airport all those years ago.

While the story has been told many times in my family, I retell it here as a timeless allegory in a familiar historic setting.

Retelling my story: The Warrior Matron

The Warrior Matron sat amidst the dusty arms housed in the back of the ancient building where in the old days they trained youth who hoped one day to be warriors, knights of honor fighting valiantly for their monarch and kingdom. She wandered, impatiently shouting orders to the covey of servants. Occasionally she'd sit and reminisce, indulging herself in visions of her past triumphs and the accomplishments of former students.

Returning from her reverie she took up her wandering again. "So much has changed in the kingdom these past few months," she thought.

Indeed the entire kingdom was in a bit of frenzy. The Warrior Matron was retiring after decades of devoted service and the Queen was relinquishing her throne to accompany her husband on the farm near the sea. The property had been the home of the Warrior Matron and her husband for a quarter century and they found great joy living there. Finding herself feeling alone in this change, she welcomed the prospect of the familiar and once again being in the company of her parents and her family on the rambling old farm.

The more surprising news to the kingdom was that the Warrior Matron refused the crown and refused it for her own young grandchildren as well. Instead, the crown would go to her niece, a young woman of honor whom the royal family and royal council held in high regard.

"Indeed", she thought with a small smile, "my life began with more choices than I could appreciate at the time, and now I recognize but a few."

The Matron's teaching days were over. She had known the day would come when she could no longer demonstrate strategic use of the sword, or lift the shield swiftly to prevent blows to her armor. Now those misplaced blows left her badly bruised for weeks. Truth be told, she had become a mother figure to the future warriors of the realm, often replacing the strong, disciplined skills of the warrior with understanding, care and caution. Now all must be set right for the new Warrior Master of this institution, a distant relative of the royal family and 20 years her junior. Although a bit pompous and patronizing, he was an experienced and honored knight of the realm.

"So much to do, so much to put in place, so alone once again," her martyred heart murmured as she arose from the dusty old crate.

"Matron! News of the Warrior Master!" yelped the meekest of the young warriors-in-the-making.

The disturbance woke the Matron from her reverie, catching her off guard. With a sudden catch to her breath, she stiffly turned to face the boy, who looked up at her, seeing the brief change in her manner.

"What news, you gnat?" she growled, struggling to regain her composure. The young man cowered, mumbled, and barely raised his nose to the light. She stepped up to him aggressively, her toes almost touching his own. He stiffened and tried to gulp, but his heart was lodged firmly in his throat.

"Eyes front!" she hissed. The boy's head adjusted itself on a spindly neck connected to a quivering body.

"Is this how a warrior stands before his Matron to report news of importance?" she demanded.

Snapping to proper attention, his chest grew as he inhaled loudly and reported, "Matron, the Warrior Master is sighted in Edmond Town. He will be here by mid-day, ma'am."

"Very good," she replied. "Gather the warriors and make ready to greet the new Warrior Master," the Matron ordered. He strode off confidently to dispatch the Matron's orders.

The Matron returned to her own chambers and closed the door. She leaned back on the strength of the heavy gilded door, took a breath and began to pace nervously.

"The Master arrives a day early!" she said with dismay. "Why didn't I see this coming? What a lack of respect for me and for the institution! Is it his intent to disgrace me by catching us unprepared? Does he intend to pack up 'the old matron' and usher her off to her unimportant pursuits?"

Her stomach roiled uncomfortably as she paced. Her bronzed leathery hands, fingers slightly bent and curled, clasped one another as she paced. She paused, imagining she heard the Warrior Master's horses in the compound, bellowing orders, taking possession of her home. The taste of fear, bitter and dry in her mouth, brought her to her senses. She inhaled deeply, braced herself, and demanded her mind to stop such thinking. It took effort, but the Matron began to gather herself, her heart supporting her resolve with each strong beat. With clarity, she knew what she must do.

Moving to her favorite chair by the fire the Matron counseled her heart: "First, face the truth. Leaving my lifelong work is a reason for the fear, and it is not welcome." She straightened her posture in her chair.

"Second, recall the early lessons. Dear heart, though I am Warrior Matron, I am alone, and this step into my future leaves me weak and fearful. I feel unprotected and vulnerable. I beseech you, dear heart, to stay calm. Be strong. Know that we are never alone." The Matron closed her eyes and spoke intently.

"Lastly, arm the warrior within," she continued, more relaxed now.

"What use is it to have lived such a rich and glorious life, if I do not use the tools that have brought me success? My armor, shield and sword protected me in battle, they'll protect me now."

She rose from her chair and knelt by the fire. Clasping her hands to her heart, she whispered, "I require the strength and resolve of my Father and Mother."

* * * * * * * * * * * * * *

Forty years earlier, the young warrior's heart had been full of awe and happiness. The world had changed, providing her with choices. She was free, a rare state for women of her station, and had chosen to become a warrior of the realm, to stand among the heroes who kept the kingdom safe and the queen protected. The bold choice had both frightened and excited her. Impatiently anticipating the ceremony and blessing before her parents, she wished instead to skip the upcoming festivities of the day and just grab her battle gear and go. However, hardheaded as she was, the young warrior recognized that the ceremony, complete with its pomp and circumstance, signaled movement from one life stage to the next.

The day of farewell was indeed lovely, decorated with morning sunshine that cast diamonds in the dew on the grass and on the leaves of the great trees. A mild breeze greeted the castle's servants as they bustled about preparing for the farewell rituals.

"Lord, I hate these blasted ceremonies," grumbled the Prince Consort, dismounting from his powerful white steed. He had been an honored knight of the realm, known throughout the kingdom as the Royal Knight, a title fitting his proud demeanor. In honor of the occasion he had dressed in his finest armor. Helmet in hand he walked confidently toward his waiting daughter, having rehearsed the words to bid her good journey. Her poise stopped him mid-stride, and as he gazed at her, pride swelled within his heart. She turned toward him, tentatively at first, and then almost imperceptibly mirrored his strong posture as she greeted him.

The Prince Consort handed his helmet to his daughter. She noted its weight and the change in her father's demeanor as he gently placed his hands over hers. They stood holding the helmet together. She looked into in his eyes, warmed by the pride beaming back at her.

"My girl, you are your mother's daughter," he said gently.

As her heart absorbed his words, she felt his bristled face buss her cheek, the weight of the helmet lifting from her hands. He placed it in the crook of his arm, stood squarely before her and held her eyes, warrior to warrior.

"As you begin this journey, you should know this, daughter: I trust your judgment," he said simply.

"M'lady, the Queen is asking for you."

"Coming," the young warrior answered, absent-mindedly. Watching her father join a group of dignitaries she was suddenly aware of her deep love for him.

Barely recognizable with dirt on her nose, a straw bonnet shading her perspiring face, and dressed in a heavy hide gardening apron and old work boots, the Queen barked orders as usual.

"Don't step on the plants, for goodness sake! We'll need more of the potatoes and carrots. And take this. Make sure everything is rinsed this time," she said as she chose the vegetables for the evening meal.

In an effort to get her attention, the young warrior tried to match her mother's movements, but the Queen was so engrossed in her gardening that she accidentally stepped backward and toppled her daughter right into the manure pile.

"Your Majesty?" the young warrior yelped.

Startled by sudden recognition, the Queen reached for her daughter. "Goodness, child! Get out of that muck, what in heaven's name is the matter with you?"

"T'was the Queen's girth that landed me here, ma'am," the young warrior teased.

"Don't be impudent! Come here!" The Queen lovingly embraced her sweet daughter with vigor as her lady's maids waddled and clucked about them, determined to untangle the royals and pull them from the mire. Soon they were immersed up to their earlobes in rose petal-scented water heated to the perfect temperature.

"Mother?"

"Yes, dear?"

"Will you miss me?"

"Oh child, I have a kingdom to look after, as well as your brothers and sisters. And of course, there is your father. Bothersome though he may be, he takes up a great deal of my heart. Despite all this, my girl, my heart longs for you already."

They turned toward one another, exchanging the warmest of smiles.

"You'll do well, my love," the Queen said simply, then allowed herself to relax in the warm water. Tears welled in the young warrior's eyes and her soul was at peace.

* * * * * * * * * * * * * *

The regiment of young warriors marched into the compound and into the Queen's presence. Priests tossed out prayers to open hearts. Storytellers regaled the spectators with ancient tales of the great battle fought for possession of their rich and mighty kingdom. Afterward, the warriors received their battle armor and swords, each one finely crafted and carrying the Queen's seal. The swords were heavy weapons with edges that gleamed dangerously, each rumored to be sharp enough to cleanly shave the bristles off the back of a boar. Each father came forward, and one by one, lifted a sword, said a few words, then solemnly presented the weapons to his waiting warrior.

As princess, the young warrior knew that her name would be called last. Her heart pounded loudly in her chest as she was called forward. Her soul seemed to open as she approached the Royal Knight. She could see her mother, seated on her throne upon a raised dais directly behind her father. Risking a glance at the Queen, she believed she saw heartbreak in her mother's eyes.

"As heir to the throne you have chosen to honor your queen and kingdom as a warrior of the realm," her father announced to a thunderous roar from the crowd. "You have completed your training with courage and distinction. You have honored yourself, your queen, and your peers!" As the crowed roared on, servants unveiled a suit of armor and her father leaned in to whisper, "I am honored, my girl."

Her heart became full with his words, their warmth pushing away fear. She looked to her mother and saw the familiar loving smile. She blushed to see the magnificent armor, deep gray, buffed to a satin finish and decorated with a rose vine complete with thorns and the royal family's insignia at the center of the breastplate. As an honored warrior of the kingdom she would now be dressed in full battle regalia before the people of the kingdom.

"Step forward and be dressed for battle," the Royal Knight commanded. The young warrior stepped forward confidently and turned toward the now hushed crowd.

"This is the metal armor that will protect your body," her father proclaimed. "Your true armor is the knowledge that you are never alone. Feel the strength and protection of this knowledge all about you." The breastplate shone as it was set in place.

The Royal Knight then lifted the heavy shield for her to grasp and stepped aside as she bore its weight.

"This is the metal shield that will deflect the blows meant to kill you. Your true shield is the calm and clear mind that keeps fear at bay. Fear seeks your weakness." He stepped forward quickly, forcefully striking the shield with his forearm. Successfully she deflected the sudden blow.

The Royal Knight presented the sword next. "This sword is your right hand. In battle it is the weapon of destruction." He placed his hand on the hilt of his own sword and said, "Your true sword is your intent, so act with thought." He drew his sword, swung it high and she skillfully blocked the mighty blow.

"Bravo!" The roar of celebration erupted among the regiment of warriors and the ceremony was over.

"Matron, your parents have arrived at the castle. The Warrior Master and his entourage are sighted and should enter the compound within the hour." The Warrior Matron was startled by the voice of her lady in waiting, and brought back to the present task of dressing for the Master's arrival. The lady guided her to the dressing table and deftly anchored a headpiece of roses in place on the Matron's head. It was heavy, she noted, but not as heavy as the helmet her father once placed in her hands.

The Matron rose and her ladies removed her robes to reveal the ivory silk jumper that protected her skin from the uniform she would don for today. They helped her step into soft leather leggings and the deep gray tunic that encased her from neck to thigh. As her ladies worked, she gazed at her own reflection, the familiar royal insignia protecting her heart, and trailing vine and rose buds decorating her shoulders.

"This is your armor, Matron," she murmured to herself. "It represents the knowledge that you are never alone. Feel the strength and protection of this knowledge all about you." The tunic fit her well. The Matron placed her hands upon her heart and felt strength well up within her.

The ladies brought her jewel case and decorated the Matron, as was customary, with the medals and insignia earned in battle. Next, they encased her forearms in beautifully crafted armor bands. Made from the same deep gray metal as her storied armor, the set had been presented to the Matron by her warriors. The left guard was decorated with the insignia of the royal family, while the right bore a vine with leaves and thorns. Both had good weight and balance and were buffed to a satin finish. She raised them over her chest, right over left and intoned softly, "These bands are my shield, a symbol of the calm, clear mind that skillfully deflects the fear that seeks my weakness."

With a slight smile gracing her face, the Warrior Matron placed her hands on her hips anticipating the weight of her sword. The scabbard rattled as the ladies arranged the finely tooled leather holding her sword and wrapped it at the Matron's waist to hang on her left hip.

Finally stepping into her boots, she felt complete. She stepped forward and drew the sword swiftly, lashing it up toward the ceiling. Her ladies scattered, frightened by the sudden aggression. Bringing the sword down slowly, she held it in her hands and gazed at it for a moment. Her ladies looked at one another, unsure of what was about to happen. The Matron lifted the sword, looking boldly into the mirror.

"This sword is your right hand. In battle it is the weapon of destruction." She felt afresh the boom of her father's voice and the warmth of her mother's loving gaze, as if 40 years had not passed. Sliding the sword back into its beautifully etched scabbard, she walked to the window and looked out upon the distant fields that sprawled around the great castle.

"In life your true sword is your intent. Act with thought," her father had said. The Warrior Matron returned to the mirror and gazed at her reflection.

"What is your intent, M'lady?" she asked. For a moment all stood still and silent. With a determined stride, the Warrior Matron stepped through the door ready to greet the new Warrior Master. It would now be his responsibility to protect the kingdom. Her days of preparing warriors were over, but her life had just begun.

* * * * * * * * * * * * * *

In my experience, the fork in the road is an uncomfortable stop; fear comes disguised as "the dreaded unknown" and time seems to stand still while others around me continue to progress. I have come to realize that such stopping points provide me time to rest; time to think before deciding on one direction or another.

Although I have never written before, this exercise in which I expressed my current career challenge by retelling it as an allegory helped me to objectify my thoughts and to feel the depth of my recollected milestones. I credit this exercise with aiding my movement forward toward new goals and the right life changes for me. In doing so, I left my job and am now helping others just like me (and you) to make important life transitions toward happiness and life fulfillment.

Questions for reflection:

So, now it's your turn to experience the value of recollection. What is your favorite analogy about life? Use it to explore the four steps:

- What is your current challenge?

- Write about a past achievement that was important to you.

- Breathe deeply and relax, then relive and honor that experience. Recapture the moment in time and record the details as you recall them. Slowly recollect and identify the specific thoughts, feelings and actions that created the moment and the outcome.

- Communicate the power and inspiration that your milestone holds for you. What method of communication would you like to explore? How do you weave your own analogy into your recollection? What creative medium motivates you today? What kind of support do you need?

I encourage you to present your recollection in a way that is meaningful and rich to you. The energy you generate from this re-creation will empower you as you meet today's challenges.

About Yvonne Anello

Yvonne Anello, CPC is a Certified Whole Person Coach with For Your Life Only. She earned her CPC at the Baraka Institute in Portland, Oregon. Her career in state government, as well as the weight-loss and worker's compensation fields, provided a solid background in teaching, management, customer service and sales.

An Oregonian with a passion for living a vital, healthy and active life, Yvonne is an optimist with an enthusiastic spirit. She has come to understand the obstacles and hurdles that often stand between an individual and their goals.

Yvonne graduated magna cum laude from Georgian Court University, in Lakewood, New Jersey with a bachelors of arts in education.

www.foryourlifeonly.com

About our Coaches

YES! We are Better Together

You are unique. And your skills, strengths and gifts can become exponentially more powerful with the support and guidance of others – providing the special edge that enables you to make any life transition achievable. At the Baraka Institute our uniqueness stems from an understanding and utilization of the best practices related to collaborative, transformative learning.

One of our guiding principles is based on the quote, "Anyone can reach success and achieve their goals." But we take it a step further. We've found the secret to accelerating personal and professional excellence is partnership (no matter what your desired outcome might be). And those who partner with mentors and guides can achieve their goals in just a few days, whereas others may take years on their own to realize the same level of positive transformation.

The Baraka Institute offers a unified network of professionals that support your goal-achievement process, making it far more effective and, of course, more fun along the way! Our coaches understand the power of a professional coaching relationship and its ability to transform dreams into reality. As a result, they're well-versed in the capacity to make change manageable and doable for you, regardless of your destination.

A Whole Person Coach works in partnership with clients, exploring goals, beliefs, resources, visions, values, attitudes, perceptions, life choices, habits and barriers. In addition, Whole Person Coaches help their clients discover and access their unique talents, abilities, passions, desires and sense of purpose. In doing so, they enable them to manifest holistic unity, personal fulfillment and comprehensive success in life.

The authors you'll find in this book are all past graduates of our program – each bold enough to step up and share their personal and professional pathways. Some of the stories reflect deeply personal journeys where others have chosen to anonymously share the journey of past clients. We're proud of these contributors and their willingness to lend their experience in support of others, knowing that together we will always find our way.

If one or more of the authors intrigues you with their story or personal perspective, we invite you to learn more by connecting with them directly through the respective websites provided at the end of each chapter.

About Baraka Institute

The Baraka Institute is a cooperative playground for the development of human potential. It's a place where exploration and learning never end. That's because we believe lifelong learning is the key to self-renewal – a pursuit that refreshes one's mental, physical, emotional and spiritual energies. Baraka makes a supreme effort to provide a safe, nurturing environment that is equally appropriate for both personal and professional transformation. Within the richness of the Baraka Institute, you'll not only receive the tools and mentorship you need to effect positive change in the world, you'll also obtain the guidance and skills you need to succeed in the business of change.

Our Guiding Principles & Mission

To live out loud, fully engaged in life and all its possibilities

At the Baraka Institute, we honor the notion of living and loving out loud – fully owning one's ideas, thoughts and dreams while respecting, trusting and honoring those of others. We are known for the value of our training and the diverse, supportive community that has formed around our guiding principles. We believe in co-creating sustainable change. We believe in continual reflection and renewal. And most importantly, we believe in a commitment to the values of awareness, action through self-empowerment, and accountability in every aspect of our personal and professional lives.

To be informed, connected and supported

Here at the Baraka Institute, we stay connected, informed and responsive to the needs of our coaches and graduate coaches. We're always here for you. Year after year, the Baraka community continues to grow bigger and stronger, developing as collaborative participants on our planet and holistically supporting the vital life forces that connect all people and our earth. We live by demonstration and being true to our whole selves. As a result, others witness the joys and opportunities that our path offers and partner with us to experience the same levels of personal and professional success.

About Whole Person Coaching

Whole Person Coaching views individuals and systems as integrated wholes, with the attention given to one's relationship to self, other people and the world serving as a lens through which to see personal strengths and opportunities.

Whole Person Coaching seeks to provide the client with access to and understanding of their WHOLE SELF in relation to their desired outcome. Whole Person Coaching is a process of pattern recognition and pattern transformation in the areas of one's life, in particular their experiences in alignment with a greater truth and capacity. By identifying the patterns in one's thoughts, feelings, communication techniques and actions, an individual can understand the underlying forces that maintain a pattern of habit and shift any pattern toward a new or enhanced outcome.

Whole Person Coaching integrates the power of the mind with the inner-knowing of the body and heart. It's based on the philosophy that, when holistically balanced and living the life that suits their individuality, people are best able to achieve their soul's purpose.

The beauty of Whole Person Coaching is the way it supports a client in the process of attaining their desired outcome – providing the tools and techniques to realize their goals more rapidly and sustain the life-enhancing changes they've made for the rest of their lives.

Learn more about us: www.BarakaInstitute.com
www.CoachTrainingWorld.com

11644382R00123

Made in the USA
Charleston, SC
11 March 2012